INNOVATION FOR EXCELLENCE

The Paracollege Model

D1263896

J. Wesley Brown

UNIVERSITY
PRESS OF
AMERICA

Lanham • New York • London

Library of Congress Cataloging-in-Publication Data

Brown, J. Wesley, 1936–
Innovation for excellence : the Paracollege model / by J. Wesley Browm.
p. cm.
Bibliography: p.
1. St. Olaf College. Paracollege—History. 2. Education,
Humanistic—Minnesota—Northfield—Case studies. 3. Educational
innovations—Minnesota—Northfield—Case studies. 4. Education,
Higher—Aims and objectives. I. Title.
LD4827.S665P373   1988   88–30208 CIP
ISBN 0–8191–7244–8 (pbk. : alk. paper)

This book is dedicated to the students and faculty

of the Paracollege

past,

present,

and

future.

89-1990

TABLE OF CONTENTS

PREFACE

This book contributes to the recurring discussion
of excellence in undergraduate education by defining
criteria by which excellence can be judged and by
describing a model by which it can be achieved. The
criteria for excellence are based on studies of effective colleges and universities done during the last
thirty years. The model is not hypothetical, a dream
college, but is one that has operated for nearly twenty
years at St. Olaf College, Northfield, Minnesota. The
particular excellence of this model, the Paracollege,
lies in its ability to foster development in those who
teach and study in it because it embodies those characteristics that research in higher education has identified as promoting development in students and faculty.
As such, the Paracollege has a foundation in theories
of development as well as credibility based on nineteen
years of existence.

It is my hope that this publication will be of
assistance to university and college administrators,
faculty, curriculum committees, and faculty development
officers who want to make their colleges more effective. The principles that underlie the operation of the
Paracollege are exportable to most other institutions
of higher education, and can be implemented with relatively little expense and great educational profit in
different types of institutions. The book also should
interest graduate and undergraduate students who wish
to study human development in higher education.

Although I present student development, faculty
development, curriculum development, and organizational
change in separate chapters, this is done solely to
present each topic in clear focus. My underlying
assumption is that the personal development of students
and faculty is a process in which many diverse elements
interact. Students, faculty, curriculum, and institutional structures, together with the mission, traditions, and supporting constituency peculiar to each
college interact to produce distinctive academic cultures at different institutions. It is the interaction
of these elements of academic culture, and the
differing weight and press of aspects of the culture
found on different campuses, that enable and constrain
the personal development of persons who work on those
campuses. (This viewpoint has been developed in an
earlier work to which I contributed, Academic Culture
and Faculty Development, Freedman et al., 1979.) My

perspectives on student and faculty development, and on academic culture, are derived from studies conducted while I was at The Wright Institute, Berkeley, and at the Center for Research and Development in Higher Education in Berkeley, California in the late 1960's.

In this book I draw on data about the Paracollege that have been collected since the first year of its existence, 1969, by the Office of Educational Research at St. Olaf College. I have also made use of a study of the Paracollege done as part of a larger study of several institutions by Robert Pace at U.C.L.A., and on studies of students, faculty, and alumni that I conducted during my six year term as Senior Tutor of the Paracollege.

In Chapter One I propose criteria by which the excellence of an educational institution may be evaluated, and set the book in the context of the current discussion of the purposes of higher education in this country. I argue that an excellent college or university is one that affects positive personal development in the lives of the students and faculty who work in it, and relate this argument to research on the influence of academic culture on the lives of students and faculty. Readers who are particularly interested in getting an overview of the Paracollege will find it in Chapter Two. In it the Paracollege is introduced as an academic innovation that incorporates many of those elements that research has identified as being positively correlated with personal development in academic communities. The subsequent chapters on student development, faculty development, curriculum, and institutional impact presuppose familiarity with the innovation described in Chapter Two. The final chapter presents data from studies of Paracollege students, alumni, and faculty that support the argument made for it as an excellent setting for human development. Those interested in the data base for the book will find it presented there. Throughout the book I make use of quotations from faculty and students that illustrate the points being discussed, and refer to studies presented in Chapter Seven. The names of persons used are fictitious and the case histories sufficiently disguised to assure the privacy of the persons quoted.

The friends who have served as resources for the book are numerous. My indebtedness to my early teachers, Nevitt Sanford and Mervin Freedman, will be obvious to anyone familiar with their interests and perspectives on higher education. George and Barbara

Helling read the manuscript and improved it by their numerous comments based on their years of experience planning and teaching in the Paracollege. Alice Thomas, Director of the Office of Educational Research at St. Olaf College, read and improved the final chapter. James Farrel, Steven Polansky, and Mary Ellen Ross, tutor-colleagues at St. Olaf, provided critical comments and encouragement throughout every stage of this project. The chapter on curriculum development originated in a paper jointly written with Jim Farrell. I thank Ann Geneva, London, England, and Martine Brownley, Emory University, for commenting on parts of the manuscript. I owe special thanks to my wife, Kathiann Brown, for her patience, encouragement, and editorial wisdom.

CHAPTER ONE

EDUCATION FOR EXCELLENCE

The university's evident lack of wholeness in an enterprise that clearly demands it
cannot help troubling some of its members.
The questions are all there. They need only
to be addressed continuously and seriously
for liberal learning to exist; for it does
not consist so much in answers as in permanent dialogue.
> Allan Bloom, The Closing of the Ameri-
> can Mind, 1987, p.380

Most Americans honor education; few
understand its larger purposes. Our thinking
about the aims of education has too often
been shallow, constricted and lacking in
reach or perspective. Our educational
purposes must be seen in the broader framework of our convictions concerning the worth
of the individual and the importance of individual fulfillment....**What we must reach for
is a conception of perpetual self-discovery,
perpetual reshaping to realize one's best
self, to be the person one could be.**
> John W. Gardner, Excellence Can We Be
> Equal and Excellent Too?, 1961, p.136

The talent development view of excellence
emphasizes the educational impact of the
institution on its students and faculty members. Its basic premise is that true excellence lies in the institution's ability
to affect its students and faculty favorably,
to enhance their intellectual and scholarly
development, and to make a positive difference in their lives. The most excellent
institutions are, in this view, those that
have the greatest impact -"add the most
value," as economists would say- on the
student's knowledge and personal development
and on the faculty member's scholarly and
pedagogical ability and productivity.
> Alexander W. Astin, Achieving Educational
> Excellence, 1985, pp. 60-61

Excellence is an idea that is much like fresh air.

Its presence is exhilarating. Its absence breeds torpor. It is hard to be opposed to it. However, like the air that sustains us, it is hard to point to and say "There it is."

It is its essential yet elusive quality that has made excellence a buzz word in education for decades. Literature about education, from preschool through graduate school, points to excellence as its presumed aim. But the literature is confused, as are the conferences and conversations that produce it, by the failure to state the criteria by which excellence is determined and the domain within which it is being discussed. Two notable exceptions to this general confusion are found in John Gardner's and Alexander Astin's discussions of excellence in higher education.

Astin has pointed out the general mystification of the meaning of excellence, its too easy identification with an institution's reputation based on its financial resources, or the selectivity of its admissions policy (Astin, 1985). Gardner has reminded us in his masterful essay, <u>Excellence</u> <u>Can</u> <u>We</u> <u>Be</u> <u>Equal</u> <u>and</u> <u>Excellent</u> <u>Too?</u>, that excellence is not just one thing. Excellence can refer to comparisons between persons, or comparisons between one's own best and worst performances. Excellence may be determined by comparative performance on normed tests on a particular subject. Or excellence may be judged by one's ability to integrate ideas in original ways (Gardner, 1961).

Excellence in a college has been determined, for example, by the percentage of graduates who earn PhD's within six years after graduating, and by the percentage of graduates who are gainfully employed a year of graduating. Might it not also be usefully determined by the percentage of students who do not require psychiatric help within six years of graduating, or even before graduating? The excellence of college programs has been determined in recent years by such means as polls of college presidents who nominate the nation's top colleges (the way sports writers rank football teams). Excellence has even been determined by counting the number of varsity athletes who eventually earn degrees from the schools they played for, (instead of how often their school's teams appeared in post season tournaments and bowl games.) Excellence, as degree of satisfaction, can be judged by the percentage of alumni who report that if they had a second chance at their college education they would repeat their experience rather than change colleges or fields of study. Discussion of excellence in education, without reference to the criteria and domain being discussed, is like measuring height with a rubber ruler. You get numbers but little meaningful information.

Some of the appeal of Allan Bloom's book, <u>The Closing of the American Mind: How Higher Education Has Failed Democracy and Impoverished the Souls of Today's Students</u>, lies in the clarity with which he articulates his idea of excellence. Bloom argues for a particular kind of excellence in higher education, an excellence in soul making whose absence he mourns. Further, his book answers the question Gardner posed in the title of his book; no, we cannot be equal and excellent too. Bloom's published lament is valuable precisely because of the vigorous responses it has elicited, responses that have renewed the discussion of the fundamental purposes of higher education in this country and that examine the criteria by which education should be judged as failing or succeeding, as mediocre or excellent.

Two years before Bloom's book was published Alexander Astin had already provided a thorough critique of the fuzzy notions that surround the idea of excellence in higher education . Astin carefully exposed the circularity of the arguments that excellence is determined by institutional reputation and resources. (Reputation is based on resources; resources accrue to institutions with good reputations; neither reputation nor resources addresses what an institution actually <u>does</u>.) Neither does judging the excellence of an institution in terms of educational outcomes answer the question, unless the students' ability at graduation is measured against their ability at entrance and significant improvement is noted (Astin, 1985).

My book is an oblique rejoinder to Bloom and an affirmation of Gardner's thesis that higher education **can** serve the democratic aims of equality and excellence. I assert with Gardner that higher education must further "self-discovery [and] perpetual reshaping" in quest of "the best self, the best person one can be." These are appropriate aims for every student and every teacher. I concur with Astin's proposal that the development of talent should be the measure of institutional excellence. The criterion by which the worth of an educational institution should be assessed is how effectively it enables the process of self-discovery and development by all those who study and teach there. Such a criterion honors the equality of persons while fostering the achievement of each individual's particu-

3

lar excellence.

The Paracollege is an innovation in higher education that responds to Gardner's concern for individual development and fulfillment. Indeed, it takes the students' and teachers' personal sense of fulfillment as one of the criteria for assessing its worth, its excellence as a model. Who better than oneself can attest to the experience of perpetual self-discovery and realization? Education for individual development in the Paracollege, however, is not antithetical to academic rigor or to the classical tradition that sees human nature as fulfilled within human community. Rather, the Paracollege supports the view that self and community are mutually constituted, that hard work in order to accomplish shared goals is fundamental to personal and community development. In our view, self and community arise and develop together or fail together in accordance with the constraints and supports that limit or enable their interaction. Thus, students' and teachers' alienation in their work reflect both the individual's failure to create meaning and the academic community's failure to provide a coherent context within which meanings can be made. In this, of course, academia mirrors the larger society of which it is a part.

That students should find a sense of fulfillment and meaning in their education is no small matter. Many of us remember, along with Bloom, that it was merely twenty years ago that students closed their campuses to protest among other things, the pointless, meaningless, anonymous routinization of their education. (Some of us remember, unlike Bloom, that those who led many of those demonstrations were among the brightest, best, ethically concerned and sensitive students of those years). A subjective sense of meaning and fulfillment is necessary. Without it there is no education at all worthy of the name, but rather a withering of curiosity and a spiritless compliance with imposed routines. However, although they are necessary, subjective standards are hardly sufficient criteria of academic excellence. Objective criteria are needed as well; but those criteria can be applied only when there is agreement, or at least a working consensus, about what the purposes of higher education are.

In our time the presumed purposes of the college or university--to produce knowledge, to teach students, and to serve society--have become mooted. The production of knowledge is driven by granting agencies, public and private, that disperse funds based on their judgement of the fit between the applicant's proposal and their guidelines, and on the agency's judgement of the applicant's ability to accomplish the proposed research. "What is Agency X funding **this** year?" is a necessary question for scholars interested in the production of knowledge. However, this flavor-of-the-month selection procedure effectively skirts the more basic issue of what larger ends research might further. It makes doubtful even the possibility of a disinterested quest for knowledge. (Faculty need those grants to do research to publish papers to keep their jobs and gain promotion.) Further, it puts in the hands of the granting agencies the power to decide what research "serves society," decisions that change with the political winds and the membership of governing boards.

That leaves the teaching of students as the area of the faculty's work most under their own control, and even this island of conscientious effort is under siege as the assumptive standards of the academic profession shove it toward the corners in even the traditional, small, liberal arts colleges. The assumptive world of the academic professional, as described by Gene Rice (1986), took form in the 1960's when federal money for research, sabbatical leaves, professional travel, and faculty mobility characterized faculty life. It was under these conditions that our image of the academic professional was formed, and colleges shaped their hiring, tenure, and promotion policies with this image in mind. As Rice points out, the values implicit in this image also shaped the faculty's idea of what it means to be a professional while these teachers were still in graduate school. The image of what it means to be excellent in the teaching profession is based on these assumptions:

1. Research is the central professional endeavor and the focus of academic life.
2. Quality in the profession is maintained by peer review and professional autonomy.
3. Knowledge is pursued for its own sake.
4. The pursuit of knowledge is best organized according to discipline (i.e., according to discipline-based departments).
5. Reputations are established through national and international professional associations.
6. The distinctive task of the academic professional is the pursuit of cognitive truth (or cognitive rationality).
7. Professional rewards and mobility accrue to

those who persistently accentuate their specializations.
Rice, p. 14, 1986

Noteworthy by its absence from this list is any explicit mention of teaching; only a generous mind would argue that the teaching of students is even implied. What this typically means for the vast majority of faculty whose institutions lack the means to support them in the pursuit of professional excellence, so defined, is that they live with a sense of personal frustration as professionals, or shame for never having "measured up" to the standards of their profession. Young faculty, especially, may flog themselves forward, usually at great cost to their families, some cost to their students, and enormous stress to themselves to succeed in the assumptive world of the academic professional while they prepare and teach a full load of courses. There is little relief or comfort for them, either, if their college has not considered what the meaning of excellence is at an institution with **its** particular financial and physical resources and teaching responsibilities. If an academic culture praises teaching, but builds its reward structure around research and publishing, teaching will suffer. A college's uncritical adoption of the assumptive values of the academic profession as its standard of excellence not only puts its faculty at risk, but its students as well. Each college must define criteria for excellence that are appropriate to its particular resources and mission, as well as to its membership in the larger academic culture. In most cases this will require discussion of the fundamental purposes of teaching at that college, and bringing that institution's system of supports and rewards in line with those purposes.

Fundamental to any such discussion is acknowledgement that education seeks to effect change in students, change in the ways in which they conceive of themselves and their world, and change in the ways in which they interact with the world. Undergirding every coherent curriculum are value assumptions, sometimes tacit, sometimes explicit, about what kinds of changes are desirable. If its graduates' sense of fulfillment and self-development is one criterion by which a college should be evaluated, a second criterion should be the success it has in fostering in students those changes that it believes are desirable. Astin calls this the "talent development" model of excellence (Astin 1985). Different kinds of institutions will seek different kinds of changes (or even in some cases to prevent change). That diversity is appropriate in a pluralistic society, but every institution should clarify and publicly state the kinds of changes it seeks.

The excellence of a liberal arts college can be measured by the effectiveness with which it increases its students' ability to think critically and complexly about themselves, their society, and their world. An excellent college will develop its students' ability to write and speak clearly, and increase their understanding of their particular aptitudes and limitations. It will enable them to acquire skills and perspectives they need in order to assume responsibility for their lives and their part in the life of their community. It will help them develop perspectives and tools with which they can analyze their society, and it will encourage them to imagine ways in which their society can be improved. Some of these criteria can be assessed as students complete their studies at a given college. (We can administer tests for breadth of knowledge as well as for cognitive complexity when they enter and when they leave the college.) Other changes can be assessed only by longitudinal studies of alumni and reports of their achievements. While success in effecting change is a useful criterion by which to measure the influence of a college, it is difficult, perhaps impossible, to attribute those changes solely to the influence of life in college, since so many other factors also impinge on youth during their college years. However, the linking of research findings that indicate substantive change in the college years with subjective self-reports that attribute much of that change to experience in college must be given some credence.

The use of such criteria is no new idea in higher education. Nevitt Sanford (1962) argued for such a definition of educational excellence twenty-five years ago. That teaching undergraduates can have developmental impact on teachers, however, has had less recognition. Academic culture has generally defined an excellent institution for faculty as one in which there are limited teaching loads, institutional support for research, talented graduate assistants, a successful grants office, and a generous sabbatical leave policy. In short, academic culture officially supports the assumptive world of the academic profession. While not wishing to deny the importance of these supports for faculty development, I will argue that an excellent educational program for undergraduates will be an excellent program for faculty development as well.

In _Academic Culture and Faculty Development_, (Freedman, et al., 1979) we noted how academic cultures differ from institution to institution, and that the "excellence" of one kind of academic culture can constrain and limit the development of faculty members whose values or personal and professional agendas are not congruent with the culture of that institution. In the 1950's and 1960's teachers had an easier time moving from campus to campus to find an academic culture hospitable to their values. Today, however, faculty have lost the easy mobility that characterized the profession in earlier decades, and institutions have responded with a variety of faculty development programs designed to stimulate and revitalize their teachers. I commend such programs, but find they are less necessary where faculty are in daily stimulating and vital contact with students, even undergraduate students. A college that effects excellence in its students can do so for its faculty as well. We have come to know a good deal about the characteristics of such effective colleges in recent years.

Ever since the publication of Nevitt Sanford's _The American College_ (1962) students of higher education have had access to research regarding the changes wrought by colleges, for better or for worse, on the lives of students and faculty. The work of Feldman and Newcomb (1969), Chickering (1969), and Astin (1977) extended and refined the work reported by Sanford, and in 1981, Chickering's _The Modern American College: Responding to the New Realities of Diverse Students and a Changing Society_ presented a comprehensive look at contemporary academic culture in this country. Astin's _Achieving Educational Excellence_ followed four years later. While the studies reported in these books were underway, an experiment in undergraduate education was going on at St. Olaf College that embodied many of the characteristics and qualities that these authors identified as essential to furthering development in both students and faculty.

The experiment at St. Olaf was called the Paracollege, an unfortunate choice of name, given the implications of "not quite the real thing" that are associated with the prefix "para." But it is my argument that the Paracollege, despite its unpromising name, has become "the real thing," an institution that has profound influence on the personal development of the faculty and students who work in it. Indeed, although it was not consciously designed as an experiment in developmental education, it has come, nonetheless, to embody those characteristics that Sanford, Feldman, Newcomb, Heath, Chickering, and Astin have identified as distinguishing colleges that produce great change in their students. The Paracollege is proof that excellence in undergraduate education is not impossible, nor is it beyond the scope of most American colleges and universities, despite Bloom's anguished cries to the contrary. Excellence, defined by students' subjective satisfaction with the college experience and measured by developmental changes in students and faculty can be achieved.

CHAPTER TWO

WHAT IS THE PARACOLLEGE?

My preference is for a tutorial system where students would report regularly to a tutor, and the tutor, say, in English literature or economics, would lead a group in a discussion of the questions raised. Each student would be geared to his own pace, going as fast or as slowly as his abilities and energy permitted. He would work on his own, using the assignment sheets of his tutors, and taking examinations at stated times....Excellence would be the standard. Full development of the idiosyncrasies of the individual would be the aim. The tutorial system would eliminate the levelling influence of the college. The tutorial institution would be aimed not at standardizing ideas, but at releasing the creative potential of every individual.
William O. Douglas, Supreme Court Justice
Autobiography,Go East Young Man,
(1974)   p.112

When you're not in the mainstream of education, when you are doing your own creating, you find that values tend to be a little different....Paracollege is a way of thinking; a synthesis of life events, of learning and of individual interests. It's an ongoing process that started in the Paracollege and will continue throughout my life.
Janell Baran, Senior Class, 1986

The best thing Paracollege did for me was make me distinct from the great herd of BA's...In my earlier job interviews, primarily in the insurance industry, employers invariably commented upon my Paracollege experience as a sign of initiative and independence ...When I interviewed with the firm I presently work for, it appeared impressed with the concept of the Paracollege. It was looking for someone who, though inexperienced, would not have to be led by the hand all summer. On the whole, I feel Paracollege was the best thing I've done for myself.
Ann Newhall, Attorney, Paracollege graduate, 1973

The system of education that Justice Douglas preferred has been practiced at the St. Olaf College
Paracollege for nearly two decades. The benefits of
this system, that arise from its attention to the
individual potential of each student and its resistance
to the homogenizing character of mass education, have
been demonstrated in the lives of students in the
program and of alumni who have carried the virtues of
its influence into society. The jeremiads of Allan
Bloom (1987) seem to have begun just when this innovation in higher education was being planned. However,
rather than closing the minds of its students, the
Paracollege has proven to be a powerful model for
linking students' concern for a meaningful education
with those critical skills and personal achievements
that have characterized the Academy at its best. What
the Paracollege innovation is and how it operates is
the theme of this chapter.

HISTORY

St. Olaf College, located in Northfield, Minnesota,
was founded in 1874 by Norwegian Lutheran emigrants to
provide an education for young men and women that would
combine academic excellence with the Christian faith
and the concerns of Scandinavian Lutheran tradition.
St. Olaf maintains to the present day both its mission
as a college of the Church and a particular interest in
the heritage of its Norwegian forebears. For many years
St. Olaf thrived as steadily increasing numbers of
students were drawn by the quality of education it
offered in the atmosphere of a caring community. By the
mid 1960's, however, the college had grown to about
2500 students, a number that necessarily strained the
very sense of community that drew students to the
college. How might the college grow without losing the
benefits of a small community? Further, how might the
college emphasize the coherence, wholeness, and integration of knowledge among its students? Those questions, and the problems that would attend their answers, had been the focus of study by a group of enter-
prising faculty at the college a decade earlier. (Hong,
et al., 1956). It was clear even then that the disciplines that had been the means for acquiring knowledge
had also become the forms in which knowledge was divided, packaged, and delivered. Any sense of the unity
of knowledge was being lost. The task of the student as
the integrating, knowing subject was obscured. The
innovation that has become the Paracollege was nurtured
in the research and writing of this group before the
experimenting ethos of the sixties brought these issues

to national attention. It was the happy concurrence of the advancement of these faculty to positions of authority in the college at the very time that innovation in American higher education was making headlines that kindled the spirit of innovation at St. Olaf.

The 1960's was a decade in which other colleges also tried to cope with the problems of expanding enrollments, fragmenting knowledge, and dissenting students. One solution attempted at several campuses was to establish smaller colleges in association with the larger college or university. These satellite colleges, or cluster colleges as they were called on some campuses, had a variety of forms of governance, mission, curriculum, admissions policies, and relationships with their sponsoring institutions. Some of these experiments in the 1960's had short, turbulent histories truncated by economic malnutrition, charismatic exhaustion, or ideological inflexibility amounting to suicide. In other cases the innovations served a short-term need of their founders and were quietly absorbed into the body of the college, or were gently put to sleep when those needs were no longer pressing.

St. Olaf learned some lessons from the battles won and lost by these earlier ventures with alternative colleges. It heeded the advice of two scholar-veterans of those fascinating years, Warren Bryan Martin, Provost of the first cluster college at University of the Pacific, Raymond College, and Jerry Gaff, one of the first Raymond College faculty and a scholar in the field of higher education. It also drew on the wisdom of members of its own faculty who had experience in the colleges of Oxford, England, and who respected the administrations' determination that whatever form the innovation took at St. Olaf, it would express uncompromisingly the college's commitment to the liberal arts. It was this combination of scholarship, experience, need, consultation, and vision that laid the foundation for the innovation begun in 1969 under the unpromising name, the Paracollege.

THE STRUCTURE

The Paracollege was consciously constructed to avoid the pitfalls that had proven the graves of other alternative colleges; it should not establish a sub-faculty that competed with the faculty of the sponsoring college for resources, students, rewards, and attention; it should serve the whole college and be perceived as doing so; it should embody academic stan-

dards that were at least as rigorous as those of St.
Olaf college. There could be no suggestion that St.
Olaf was offering a cheap or easy degree through its
alternative college. On the other hand, it had to
acknowledge the indisputable fact that students differ
from each other in innumerable ways, a fact students in
the 1960's were finding innumerable ways to impress on
the nation's consciousness. The foundations of the
Paracollege were carefully laid to bridge these pitfalls and to sustain the weight of its serious academic
purposes. Just how this was done will be seen in the
following descriptions of the faculty, Paracollege
governance, the nature of the curriculum, and the student community.

Faculty

The founding faculty of the Paracollege were St.
Olaf teachers who, for the most part, were familiar and
respected colleagues of the faculty of the college.
Here the first ditch was dodged. The mistake of bringing "outsiders" to the campus to do something that the
college's faculty, evidently, was not talented enough
to do for itself was avoided. From the outset tutors in
the Paracollege have been selected from the departments
of the college. Each teaches a portion of his assigned
course load within the curriculum of the Paracollege. A
core of tutors teaches in the Paracollege for one-half
time. A larger number of tutors is assigned for one-
third of their course load, and a few faculty provide
tutorials in the Paracollege at one-sixth time. (A full
faculty course load at St. Olaf is six courses for the
academic year.) The Senior Tutor, the chief administra-
tor of the Paracollege, negotiates the appointment of
tutors to the Paracollege with the Chair of each tutor's department. The departments are committed to
provide tutors for the Paracollege and they take this
into account when planning their own curricula and
course assignments. This arrangement provides tutors
assigned to the Paracollege with sufficient time in the
Paracollege to give leadership to its committees as
well as assures that most departments of the college
participate in the innovation to some degree at all
times. The tutors currently number about fourteen full
time equivalents, divided among some thirty-five faculty members. Tutors expect to work within the Paracollege for a period of years and then to rotate back into
their full departmental assignments, making way for
other faculty to become Paracollege tutors.

There are many institutional advantages to making

14

appointments in this way, although it makes the administration of the Paracollege and of departments somewhat more complex. The principal advantage is that it has prevented the polarizing of the faculty into "we" and "they" divisions, which on other campuses that experimented with alternative colleges became virulent "legitimate" vs. "illegitimate", or "privileged" vs. "exploited" camps which battled for institutional resources, students, and rewards. Further, the rotation of faculty in and out of the Paracollege has important consequences for their professional development, the college's curriculum, and the institution as a whole that we will consider in more detail in subsequent chapters.

Governance

The Paracollege was charged by the administration of the college to govern itself with "limited autonomy." It is not surprising that some of the more interesting episodes in the Paracollege's history have centered on defining the limits of such an ambiguous mandate. That the whole enterprise did not die in its infancy is testimony to the patience, good will, high hopes, trust, and commitment to success on the part of all those persons involved with the innovation. What this limited autonomy has come to mean in terms of curriculum and pedagogy is that the Paracollege is free to experiment as long as its degree requirements remain "comparable" to those of the general college. As for hiring and dismissing its own faculty, the Paracollege does neither. Departments consider their need to provide tutors for the Paracollege when seeking candidates for positions at the college, and the Paracollege, in turn, provides peer and student reviews of the tutors' teaching and general work in Paracollege when faculty are evaluated for contract renewal, tenure, and promotion.

The Chair of a department and the Senior Tutor consult about the assignment of tutors to the Paracollege, discussing the needs of each and striving to offer a balanced curriculum. Faculty are not forced to become tutors; rather, teachers usually express an interest in working in the Paracollege and discuss the possibility with their colleagues who are currently teaching in the Paracollege as well as with their department's Chair and the Senior Tutor.

The Paracollege faculty, with student representation, meets as a body and in committees to deliberate and act upon matters pertaining to curriculum and staffing of the Paracollege. The Paracollege faculty seeks and nominates its own administrators, the Senior Tutor and Academic Coordinator, but these are officially appointed by the Dean of the College. The Paracollege, as such, is represented on the college committees that review curriculum and educational policy, and that review and plan matters pertaining to faculty status and benefits.

Finally, the Paracollege is authorized to seek grants, but does not pursue development funds independent of the college; its programs are funded by the central administration as are other divisions of the college.

Such arrangements make the Paracollege something other than a department, as it has no subject matter peculiar to it, and something other than a distinct school or college, as all its constituents participate in various ways in the life of the larger college. It resists being lumped or subsumed among other academic units at St. Olaf, or elsewhere for that matter. There are few cognates in higher education with which to compare it, which makes it difficult to explain. But it is perhaps this "something else" quality about it that gives it much of its value as a model. The Paracollege is a genuine working alternative to traditional course-based education that complements rather than competes with that tradition. A product now as much of evolution as of planning, the Paracollege is not the kind of innovation one is apt to think of spontaneously. But, then, neither is the camel, which has proven an invaluable servant to civilization for centuries.

Curriculum

In 1968 the Dean of the College, one of the authors of Integration in the Christian Liberal Arts College, (Hong, et al., 1956) initiated a year-long study and consultation within the faculty concerning the new college before the first students were admitted. This consultation produced a model for the Paracollege curriculum that stressed interdisciplinary, integrative, and individualized programs of study for its students.

One of the facts the planning committee sought to honor is student diversity. Fortunately, by 1969, the year of the Paracollege's inception, the individual differences of students had received sufficient attention from scholars of higher education to legitimate, indeed to require, making provision for such differences. The Paracollege curriculum serves student diversity by means of a flexible system of instruction and evaluation. Students use seminars, workshops, independent studies as well as courses to acquire a broad, integrated understanding of the humanities, social and natural sciences. But the key element in its flexibility is the ancient, conservative "innovation", the tutorial system of instruction similar to that of Oxford or Cambridge Universities. Let students study in the company of a scholar who devotes attention to their style and interests, accelerating, diverging, or pausing in order to consider a significant issue in depth; that allows for individual differences in students' previous knowledge and learning styles. But let there be no lowering of academic standards. Students' work is evaluated within the tutorials, and by teams of faculty who read the interdisciplinary, integrative papers prepared by students. Finally, in order to graduate, students must demonstrate their knowledge in a way that has been certified and respected for centuries, comprehensive examinations that require them to demonstrate their mastery of their subject specialities. That pleases the apostles of orthodoxy, and more importantly, it graces the student with an experience of gennuine accomplishment. Students and faculty together prospect and mine the riches of an American liberal arts college curriculum; the whole course catalogue, in addition to individually devised tutorials, is available to Paracollege students; that uncovers the true wealth of the _alma_ _mater_ lode, and enriches the academic experience for students and faculty alike.

There is one required course in the Paracollege. It is the year-long Freshman Seminar, the primary aim of which is to initiate students into the philosophy and procedures of the Paracollege. The philosophy is addressed explicitly in the subjects read, discussed, and written about in the seminar, and implicitly in the style in which the seminar is organized. Students read and discuss texts that provide them with a common stock of ideas, images, and issues that they will address throughout their education. There can be shared discourse only where there is a community of ideas. Students are required to write their responses to the readings and seminar discussions. That writing is carefully assessed and, itself, becomes part of the seminar's discussion. The idea is to create a forum in which students are addressed by significant ideas, and in which their own responses to those ideas are taken seriously by tutors and students alike. In the Freshman

17

Seminar we begin to establish a community of students who are more involved in working together to address issues common to them all, (e.g., what are the aims of liberal education in general, and their own education in particular) than they are in performing to please the tutors. The degree to which they succeed in doing so is the measure of their preparedness to benefit from the challenge of studies soon to come in their years as upperclass students.

The Paracollege is designed to provide opportunities for general education as well as subject matter specializations. Students are expected to acquire their general education in the social sciences, humanities, natural sciences and mathematics in seminars and tutorials specially designed to present materials in an interdisciplinary way. Because students bring varying degrees of preparation to these studies it is not expected that every student will need to take the same seminars or tutorials. Each student studies those topics each needs in order to prepare for the General Education examinations in these fields. We publish the subject areas that have to be mastered for the exams. Tutors work with students, helping them prepare for the examinations, much like coaches help their charges prepare for the challenges they must face on the athletic field. The objective is to devise a teaching arrangement wherein summative evaluation is separated from the task of teaching, in which the students experience the teacher as being unquestionably "on their side" as they prepare for the general education examinations. Students' study programs take into account what knowledge of specific areas they already have; attention is paid to strengthening areas in which students' knowledge is deficient. The General Education Examinations, offered twice yearly, may be taken when the students decide they are ready. While all of the preparatory tutorials and seminars receive narrative evaluations, only the students' performance on the examinations themselves receives a letter grade, and the examinations may be repeated by any students who wish to improve their grades.

Within each examination area the students are expected to demonstrate their ability to integrate and use the knowledge they have gained in tutorials and seminars. Simply repeating the bits of information acquired is not acceptable. For example, one part of the humanities general education examination asks students to discuss the relationships among historical events, signal ideas, the literature, philosophy, religion, and arts within a designated time period. A part of the social sciences examination requires students to demonstrate how social scientists from at least two disciplines would identify, describe, and investigate some social problem presented in the popular press.

This system of individual preparation for the general education examination was the original and, to my mind, the best method by which students acquired and demonstrated a personally integrated knowledge of the required subject areas. It was from the outset, how ever, a system that daunted prospective students. Despite attempts to emphasize its low risk (take the exam when you feel ready, and retake it until you are satisfied with your performance), and its high gain (study in order to complement areas you already know well in order to develop a coherent grasp of a period or area), students preferred to satisfy general education requirements in the familiar courses-for-distribution-method of the general college. Students, we found, were choosing to transfer into the Paracollege to pursue advanced work after having met the breadth requirements in the college's departments.

The faculty of the Paracollege responded to this reticence by revising the requirements for papers and examinations in the Paracollege general education seminars. The faculty provides interdisciplinary, general education seminars that examine fundamental ideas from the perspective of several disciplines. The seminars are team taught, providing students with models of how different disciplines approach and understand particular phenomena. Students must now do within each seminar what they would do were they to take the General Education Examinations; that is, they must write papers and examinations in which they demonstrate their own integrated understanding of the topics studied in each seminar.

For example, the humanities seminars are taught by faculty from the fields of art, history, literature, religion, music, and philosophy. A sequence of five chronological seminars (The Ancient World, The Middle Ages and the Renaissance, The Reformation, Baroque, and Enlightenment, The Nineteenth Century, The Twentieth Century) provides students with a comprehensive, interdisciplinary exposure to Western civilization. Students may satisfy the general education requirement in humanities by taking four of these seminars, or by completing personally devised study programs that include work in these seminars, college courses, and papers written in tutorials. The work done in seminars, or in these personally devised programs, must exhibit breadth and integration of thought similar to that required for the General Education Examination.

In addition to general knowledge in these broad areas of the college curriculum, students are required to have had experience in creative arts, foreign language, and physical education. In the arts, for example, as student might participate in music, dance, theater, or graphic arts of many sorts; the point is to have students involve themselves in the problems and satisfactions of artistic production. One discovers things about a subject and about oneself by practicing the art that can not be learned simply by reading or observing it. Students are required to demonstrate competence in a foreign language equivalent to at least the level of a third semester course in the language. Physical education is also required, but here again, the emphasis is upon the student's demonstrating proficiency in an activity. The range of activities encompasses those taught at St. Olaf plus many which students already practice and enjoy, e.g. cross-country skiing, canoeing, aerobics.

The religion requirement in the general college is three courses, two beyond the mandatory freshman religion course. In the Paracollege students must present evidence of comparable work, with the additional proviso that the studies must include investigation of some classic work of the Christian tradition (e.g. scripture, theology), some work that investigates the relationship of religion to culture, and a critical and constructive study reflecting the student's own assessment of the role of religion in his or her personal life.

Advanced work within the Paracollege is organized in the student's concentration. Here, again, students may study topics of interest to them in tutorials, seminars, courses in the general college, independent research, or study abroad. The students must integrate these studies around a chosen theme or problem and write comprehensive examinations over the concentration during their senior year. The concentration is often an interdisciplinary effort. For example, recent concentrations have been in Environmental Studies, The Nuclear Family in a Nuclear Age, Psychology and Art, The Idea of the Self in Nineteenth and Twentieth Century Philosophy and Literature, and The Image of Woman in Nineteenth Century Literature and Art. A committee of no fewer than three faculty members advises the student in the preparation of the concentration, administers and reads the examinations, and conducts an oral examination over the student's written examination as well. The comprehensive examinations are given both a written evaluation and a letter grade, both of which appear on the student's college transcript.

Further demonstration of the student's proficiency is required in the form of a Senior Project. This project is a major effort during the student's senior year, comparable to at least one course, and is designed to demonstrate her ability to use the skills and knowledge acquired in the development of her concentration. For example, a student whose concentration is in a fine arts area might hang an exhibition of her work, or present a recital, or direct a play as a senior project. A student in literature might present a series of essays in literary criticism. A social science concentration might include an original research project. In every case the Senior Project must demonstrate the student's proficiency in her field of endeavor, and, like the comprehensive examinations, it receives both a narrative evaluation and grade on the college transcript. A list of some recent concentrations and senior projects follows.

Twentieth Century British and American Drama and Literature
    Project: Directing the play, "The Horse Dreamer"
Political Psychology
    Project: Creation of a game simulation of the political dynamics of a developing Latin American country
Computer Science and Human Intelligence
    Project: A computer program that simulates manic-depressive personality
Film History and Practice
    Project: Writing, directing, and producing a documentary film
Environmental Studies: Perspectives East and West
    Project: Restoration of a Minnesota tall grass prairie
Creative Writing
    Project: Five Short Stories

STUDENTS

St. Olaf College enrolls three thousand students annually, and any student admitted to the college may enter the Paracollege program. About one-hundred-sixty students enroll each year in the Paracollege degree program, and an additional three hundred students from the general college register for one or more of the interdisciplinary seminars offered by the Paracollege faculty. Most students who enter the Paracollege have come to St. Olaf because of its reputation as a fine institution. Most students who enter the Paracollege after they have studied for a year or two at St. Olaf do so in order to pursue interdisciplinary studies or concentrations, or because they find their learning enhanced by an educational program that takes into account their individual learning style, interests, and abilities. In addition, some students choose to come to St. Olaf because they have heard about the Paracollege and could find nothing like it elsewhere.

The Paracollege was not designed to be an honors college, nor a place for remedial work. Any student admitted to St. Olaf College is eligible to work in the Paracollege. This has been an important factor in the success of the innovation. Indeed, Paracollege has attracted some of the finest students who enroll at the college, but it has not been perceived as a "brain drain" by the departments or a haven for "eggheads" by other students. Because students work very closely with their tutors and the modes of instruction are flexible in the Paracollege, the pace, scope, and the duration of a tutorial can be adjusted to the gifts and limitations of each student. For these reasons some students are able to succeed in their education in ways simply not possible for them in a standard course and credit system. This has not made the Paracollege a refuge for students who are academically deficient. Rather, as the possibilities available for students within the Para-college have become better understood by the faculty at large, the innovation has increasingly been seen as an opportunity to serve students who have unusual gifts as well as unusual problems.

Students who are most apt to be attracted to St. Olaf because of the Paracollege are those who have felt constrained by a mechanistic, inflexible high school setting or, conversely, who have enjoyed already the advantages of a school that has respected them as individuals. Their standardized test scores at entrance are usually above the mean scores of their entering classmates. They may not yet have had great success as independent learners because of lack of opportunity, but they share an eagerness to step beyond the bounds

of the familiar, for some the all too familiar, routines of education.

Community

The hope that a college may grow larger without
losing its humane scale and sense of collegiality is a
worthy one. It is often the oppressive feeling of
neither knowing nor being known by people who surround
them that drives students to the counselors' office, or
to the variety of forms of narcotizing distraction that
abound in student culture. Students and faculty long
to establish contact with people who know them and who
care about what interests them. One would think that
would not be a problem in an intellectual community,
but it is.

The Paracollege addresses the phenomenon of
isolation within a campus on two levels, structurally
and programatically. First, the Paracollege is a
subcommunity within the larger college that provides
occasions for students and faculty from across the
departments and divisions of the college to meet
together. The teaching settings most used in the
Paracollege, seminars and tutorials, encourage close
interaction among students and faculty. Tutors and
students meet weekly in face to face, person to person
discussions of the student's work; tutorials become
opportunities for the student and tutor to explore and
study what they both care about. As we will see in
later chapters, these encounters are educationally
powerful because they challenge students and tutors to
relate to each other as distinct individuals. Seminars
and colloquia are extended investigations of a shared
interest with a larger group of students, often led
by an interdisciplinary team of teachers. Since no
seminar beyond the freshman year is required, students
who participate in them do so out of mutual interest
and commitment to the enterprise. Over the course of
semesters in the Paracollege students often recover
that spontaneity and verve that has been sacrificed to
defensive caution, that skill of never risking and
owning an idea on any subject that made survival
possible in an environment where individuals alienate
each other in competition for grades. Further, students
come to appreciate the insights of their classmates
whose contributions enrich the experience of the group.

The humanizing effect of the Paracollege touches
the lives of not only the students but of their tutors
as well. Some tutors see teaching in the Paracollege as

an enlivening respite from departmental politics. Some find the most rewarding aspect of their experience in the Paracollege to be teaching students who are studying with them in order to develop a shared interest. For some a source of stimulating communication is the interaction with colleagues from departments across the campus who bring with them new viewpoints and questions. For many reasons, these among them, faculty attest to the invigorating and sustaining sense of community they find in their Paracollege work.

Most of the activities of the Paracollege perk along in tutorials and seminars, in groups of two to twenty people. There is one regular occasion, however, on which that dismembered body of tutors and students which is the Paracollege remembers itself as a coherent community. That is at the weekly dinner shared by students, tutors, and sometimes tutors' spouses and children as well. Quite in contrast to the Oxford High Table, with its segregation of tutors from students, emphasizing by its formality of dress and proscriptive decorum the distinctions that separate those assembled, the weekly Paradinner is an opportunity to enjoy one another in the human ritual of a shared meal. In the hour and a half devoted to the dinner the Paracollege hears announcements about the activities of its members to which those assembled are invited (it might be a protest march, it might be a vocal recital, it might be a senior's oral examination, it might be a trip to the Guthrie Theater in Minneapolis). A program of perhaps forty-five minutes length follows. This might be a presentation of one of the tutors' research, or one of the students' Senior Projects. One week papers that originated in one of the seminars may find their way to Paradinner. Another week the Natural Sciences Seminar might present skits on Relative Quantum Leaps Up the Evolutionary Ladder, or some other bit of foolishness. Versions of College Quiz Bowl, pitting tutors against students, are an annual event played to standing room only. Another week the resident chess master may play a simultaneous match against all comers. Faculty who are not in the Paracollege but who wish to have a forum for their ideas may find it here. Poets and other creative writers, from the campus or the wider community, read their work for the community's enjoyment. Sometimes the program is a discussion of some educational policy under review within the Paracollege. Or it might simply be a party celebrating the graduating Seniors, or practically any other semi-defensible pretext. At Paradinner the individuals who are the Paracollege celebrate and enjoy their accomplishments, their diversity, their community.

The dinners provide an important socializing function, in both the technical and lay meanings of those words. Underclass students see and hear what seniors are doing; a generally high standard of performance is the model. Students and tutors find a wider, supportive audience for the work they have done in small groups and tutorials; the incentive to do good work is enhanced and the community comes to know its life in richer and finer detail. Friendships are made and extended. Discussions begun in seminars are continued informally around the table, often with an altered set of participants. That sense of shared enterprise that is the healthy core of community is nurtured. What those who founded the Paracollege hoped to realize by way of growth and community is taking place.

The first Paracollege tutors at the founding convocation for the Paracollege in 1969. Left to right: James Butterworth, Art; George Helling, Sociology; William Narum, Philosophy, Religion; Erling Jorstad, History, American Studies; Paul Fjelstad, Natural Science and Mathematics; David Wee, English.

William H.K. Narum, first
Senior Tutor, guided the
Paracollege from 1969-1973.

David Wee, Senior Tutor,
1971-1972, Senior Tutor
from 1976-1979.

Vernon Faillettaz, Department of
Religion, Senior Tutor from 1973-
1976.

Left: William Poehlmann, Department of Religion,
Senior Tutor from 1970-1980: Right: J. Wesley Brown,
Departments of Psychology and Religion. Brown was
Senior Tutor of the Paracollege from 1980 to 1986.

, right: Constance Geng-
ach, Department of His-
y, leading a tutorial
 her speciality, European
ellectual history. Geng-
ach developed the human-
es interdisciplinary sem-
rs and lead the Paracol-
e as Senior Tutor for
 year before her death
1987.

ht: Gary Deason, Depart-
ts of History, Philo-
hy, and Religion assumed
ies as Senior Tutor in
7 and currently leads
 Paracollege.

Paracollege tutors work with
students in diverse ways and
settings. Above, left, Mal-
colm Gimse, Art, explains a
12th century Chinese scroll.
Above, right, Gene Bakko,
Biology, helps students with
a laboratory project. Over
many cups of coffee, Paul
Kirchner, rights, leads a
student in a tutorial in
linguistics.

CHAPTER THREE

STUDENT DEVELOPMENT IN THE PARACOLLEGE

An excellent learning environment is
characterized by three conditions: student
involvement, high expectations, and assessment and feedback. Involvement is really the
corner-stone of this mini-theory in the sense
that the setting of high expectations and
provision of timely feedback are in actuality
the means for enhancing student involvement.
Alexander Astin, Change Magazine,
(July/August 1985)

Everything that lives, lives by drawing
together strands of experience as a basis for
its action; to live is to act, to move forward into the world of experience. Meaning
then - for any animal - is the drawing together of aspects of experience for action
and well-being. But psychology has shown us
that man does not draw experience together on
the basis of simple sensations, but rather,
on the basis of concepts. Man is the animal
in nature who, par excellence, imposes symbolic categories of thought on raw experience.
In other words, with man, meaning has
become conscious; his conception of life
determines how he will see all its parts.
Ernest Becker, Beyond Alienation,
p. 126, 1967.

WHAT DO WE MEAN BY DEVELOPMENT IN COLLEGE?

Virtually every college catalogue describes a serious academic community committed to cultivating among
its students high character and intellectual versatility. Some colleges are so committed. Research on the
impact of colleges on student development has done much
to help us discriminate between colleges whose cata-
logues deserve awards for creative fiction and those
that consistently do affect positive changes in their
students. The research of Astin (1977), Chickering
(1969, 1981), Feldman and Newcomb (1969), Gaff (1978),
D. Heath (1968, 1977), Pace (1979), Sanford (1968), and
Wilson and Gaff (1971), among others, converges on a
relatively small number of institutional characteristics that account for developmental changes in stu-

dents. It is these institutional characteristics and the personal development to which they are related that are my concern in this chapter. But it may be useful at the outset to lay to rest some of the misconceptions which prevent many faculty members from embracing a developmental perspective in their teaching.

Teaching with an eye to the development of students does not mean that faculty must subordinate the importance of their subject matter that they teach, or that they must develop some new bag of pedagogical tricks, or that they must take a second degree in psychology. The stock in trade of the college faculty member is ideas, ideas that are exciting and interesting to her and which she feels are important for others to know. Her excitement and her interest are an expression of her values, her commitments, her construction of her life's meaning. In teaching she shares these commitments, values, and this vision of what life can mean. She derives self-esteem, at least in part, from her ability to think, speak, and write effectively. She does not experience her life as separated into distinct compartments, one labelled "cognitive" the other labelled "affective", or "emotional." Were she to reflect upon what experiences had been developmentally significant for her, she would speak of intellectual challenges met in school, in her research, sometimes with her colleagues, often with students, usually with spouse and children. She would speak of relationships with faculty members when she was in undergraduate or graduate school that in some sense confirmed her in her identity as a scholar. Such were the thoughts faculty shared with us when we asked them about their life experience. (See Freedman, et al., 1979) Their educations did not seem "developmental" to them at the time they were studying; but in retrospect they could, indeed, identify persons, tasks, challenges, and relationships in their educational experience that had implications for who they had become far beyond the courses that were the occasion for the experience. Development, in this sense, is the significant thing that can happen to students in college while they are "earning their degree." That it happens more infrequently, haphazardly, and serendipitously than need be the case is the message that the studies of student development in college are making clear. What colleges can do, and what faculty in particular can do to increase the probability of it happening is what this book is about. But what faculty must not do is sacrifice or compromise their commitment to intellectual activity; what administrators need not do is establish programs specially directed at affective development. Such experiments are counter to the purposes of the university, are doomed to be overwhelmed by the conservative forces of academic culture, and, furthermore, are quite unnecessary.

Having struck this reassuring note I hope you will not be put off by the more detailed explanation of what I mean by development. Development of the college student, like development of any human being, involves what are called the "cognitive" and "affective " domains of that person. Development implies a person's ability to think about ideas - perhaps most importantly his own ideas - analytically. The "developed" person, in this sense, can criticise his own thought and has sufficient "distance" from his thought that he can hold it at arms length, as it were, examine it, and let others examine it, alter it, refine it, or reject it. In Robert Kegan's (1982) terms, the developed person is not embedded in his thought, but has emerged as a self to the extent that his thoughts can become objects for his own reflection. Development, then, is not the acquisition of more information; it is the ability to receive and organize more information in increasingly complex and diverse ways, and to understand its relationships to wider realms of experience.

This understanding of development asserts an intimate connection, an interdependence, between the cognitive and affective domains of the person. Indeed, it is only for purposes of description and analysis that the two, cognitive and affective, should be separated. What is cognitively perceived is dynamically related to a person's affective needs and the way he constructs the meaning of his world. For example, a student may be so emotionally dependent on his family for his sense of identity and worth that he cannot assimilate and understand an economic theory or theological viewpoint that would challenge his relationship with his family. Knowing, in this case, is hindered by fear of the consequences of knowing; his affective needs interfere with his cognitive development. To make matters worse, he is probably unconscious or only dimly aware of his emotional dependence. His conflict between needing to know and his fear of knowing may manifest itself in avoidance of study, skipping class, somatic illness, or contentiousness in and outside of class. In Kegan's formulation of this problem the student is still so embedded in the matrix of his family's meaning in his life that he cannot hold his family, with its ideas and values, sufficiently at a distance to be able to think about them critically. His problem, as far as his being a student is concerned, is not that he lacks intelligence, but that his intelligence is unavailable to the tasks of study because of his developmental immaturity.

By affective development we mean changes in the student's attitudes, aspirations, values and ways of holding to ideas that move the student toward increased capacity for complex, rational thought (Heath, 1977); in other words, a shift in the balance between the student's embeddedness in his current life's meaning toward an increased ability to emerge from that context and reflect upon it. What may perpetuate his embeddedness is his anxiety about the unpredictable consequences of adapting a new view of his world, or a sense of infidelity to his values, or a perceived threat to his sense of identity (Kegan, 1982). Greater affective development means our thinking is less dominated by our needs and emotions; we "have" our needs and emotions, as opposed to being had by them. We possess them, and to some degree know ourselves as persons apart from them. This capacity also allows us to take another person's viewpoint and understand his construction of meaning; we can see it as his, one that we may in some part share but that does not thereby invalidate or threaten our own meaning. In such a state the world of ideas becomes a realm of possibilities to which we are more open and by which we are not necessarily intimidated.

Teachers need not become psychologists in order to appreciate the interdependence of affective and cognitive elements in the development of their students. They would, however, be helped in their work as teachers if they reflected upon these factors in their own experience. Such reflection on the process of "intellectual" development can make teaching more satisfying. It can make comprehensible what is otherwise frequently baffling behavior in some students. What may appear as obtuse ignorance in students, wrong-headedness that will not yield to clearer explanations, masterful lectures, or detailed charts and bibliographies, may really be their defense against ideas that threaten their integrity, their coherence as persons. Understanding this, the teacher's frustration may be allayed. What may be needed is not another scintillating lecture over the difficult material, but perhaps the presentation of themselves as persons who can, indeed, deal with ideas and images which they admit some people may find repugnant or threatening but which need not undermine the possibility of coherent, moral personhood.

Even the earliest colleges in this country tried to foster personal development in their students. Traditionally, this development was described in moral, religious, and civic terms. The inculcation of "character" has been at least a secondary aim of higher education since the founding of colleges began in America in the seventeenth century. Churches were concerned to raise up young men fit to preach, teach, and govern in the new world (Sanford, 1964, Rudolph, 1962). The work of Perry and his followers, and of Kegan in constructive developmental psychology is refining these concerns and extending our understanding of development in the college years (Kegan 1982, Perry 1970).

Research on the impact of colleges on students has enabled us to identify those characteristics of institutions which are salient in affecting the development of "character" in their students. Colleges that are academically selective, small, private, four-year, and residential generally may be expected to have significant impact on student development (Astin 1977). This is especially the case where there is consonance between the values of the faculty and the interests of the students selected for admission to the college (Chickering 1969). But these descriptors apply to hundreds of colleges, not all of which embody the qualities essential to development in the college years. The critical factors are those noted in the first quotation at the head of this chapter: opportunities for involvement of the students with faculty; high expectations for students' performance; and assessment of students' work in ways that are helpful to them. These factors can be translated to specific kinds of opportunities for students in a college setting. These opportunities, listed in Table I, and their importance within the Paracollege are the theme of my discussion in the remainder of the chapter.

TABLE I

A learning environment is excellent if it provides opportunities for students to:
1. make choices.
2. interact with diverse individuals and ideas.
3. have direct and varied experiences in learning.
4. solve intellectual problems without having to conform to an authority's viewpoint of how it must be done.
5. be involved in the process of evaluation and self-assessment.

6. learn how to free oneself from excessive anxiety.
7. achieve goals meaningful to oneself.

MAKING CHOICES IN THE PARACOLLEGE

Students in standard college programs make "big" choices at the time of registration: what four of five courses to take, and then what topics to select for term papers. Those decisions are remade at the beginning of each term. Instead of making a variety of choices regarding what and how to study, and rationalizing those choices within a personally devised program of study, the typical college student repeats the course selection experience 36 to 40 times, depending on the number of courses required for graduation. In contrast, one of the most challenging aspects of study to the new student in the Paracollege is the choices she must make; the choices available to these students appear to be over whelming, unlimited. In fact, however, the choices available are limited by three factors: the range of expertise presented by the liberal arts faculty, the degree requirements established by the faculty, and the students' and tutors' ideas as to how these first two can be made to intersect in a way particularly fruitful to each student. Even this range of choices is considerably larger than that available to students in most college programs.

This is because the range of expertise of a liberal arts faculty is generally much larger than the limited number of courses each faculty member is assigned to teach. Most teachers have developed competence in subject areas while earning their Master's and Doctor's degrees which they reluctantly had to set aside to develop their degree specialization. Furthermore, teachers often do not have the chance to teach in the area of their specialization, and more often have no chance to teach topics they have studied and enjoyed but which are the province of more senior members in their department. In addition, intellectually vital faculty continue to read and to develop competencies they did not acquire during their years of formal schooling. This wealth of knowledge available to students in the abilities of their teachers is only hinted at in the usual course catalogue. There is no educational reason why these interests and abilities of a faculty need to lie dormant, inaccessible to students. In the Paracollege they are made available.

Paracollege tutors are the same persons who offer courses in the disciplinary departments of the general college but who are freed by the structure of the Paracollege to bring into play their broader educational interests and skills. Each Paracollege student has the college's course catalogue from which to select courses, but that range of options is expanded to include the general education seminars and topical seminars offered by teachers serving as Paracollege tutors. Further, there is the variety of topics for tutorials that teachers have indicated they are prepared to direct. To make choices even more complex, the announced tutorial subject areas, (humanistic psychology, 18th century English history, Native American religion, for example) suggest broad areas within which the tutor is prepared to teach. The student negotiates the actual topic and specific sub-topics within this broad area in conversation with the tutor. Setting up the tutorial involves the student in a number of important choices, and at the same time introduces the other opportunities to choose listed in Table I.

Choice for the Paracollege student is, therefore, much more than selection among predetermined alternatives. Choosing requires a student to devise a rationale for the proposed tutorial that makes sense in terms of the general requirements for the degree she is seeking and her own specific educational interests and objectives. Taking a tutorial because she "has to satisfy a distribution requirement," or because it can fit conveniently between two scheduled courses for her major is not enough. She must show the tutor why the study, for example, of German Expressionism will be a meaningful contribution to her education. She will need to present something of her own context for study of this topic, what she already knows about art and the relevant philosophy and social history. She may already know quite a bit about the topic, or she may have only a sketchy idea of German Expressionism gleaned from a Western Civilization course. But it is her knowledge, her questions, her interests that provide the framework within which the tutorial is begun. That framework will expand and be filled in as the tutorial proceeds, but the crucial point here is that she has had to choose a course of study that makes connections at various levels with her already existing knowledge and interests. She has had to invest her choices with meaning from the beginning.

The negotiation of the tutorial is really the initiation of a series of choices relative to the topic. Since the tutorial does not exist as a printed syllabus in the tutor's file cabinet, but develops week-to-week through the interaction of the student's questions and the tutor's expertise, the choice of a tutorial is really the introduction to an expanding network of choices in subsequent weeks. In most fields of study there are great works that should be read. But the great works have become great because of their power to expand and illuminate possibilities for thought, and it is these possibilities that become the occasion of further choices by the student in the tutorial.

A remarkable development occurs as students explore studies they have chosen and helped to define. They acquire a confidence in the validity of their own questions. They experience the desideratum of Emerson's "American Scholar," what it is to be a man or a woman thinking. Study becomes a means of intellectual expansion and emotional satisfaction, not a task imposed by a teacher in order to pass a midterm exam. The high degree of satisfaction with the Paracollege expressed by students and alumni can be attributed in large measure to their meaningful choices made all along the way.

The diversity of options and the necessity of choosing that confront the Paracollege student could be construed as mere lack of educational direction. One critic describes the Paracollege as "something of a scandal, an intellectual and pedagogical scandal in which sloppy thinking is posing as pedagogical flexibility." What such a critique fails to deal with is the success enjoyed by Paracollege students measured by even the most traditional standards. It ignores the high degree of satisfaction Paracollege students find in their studies that motivates them throughout their college careers, and the achievements within those studies that sustain them in careers and advanced degree programs. Further, it leans too heavily upon the idea that education inheres in the object studied rather than in the subject studying, a reversal of the order of things which, if it were true, would make every student of great writing a Melville and every student of mathematics a Russell.

INTERACTION WITH DIVERSE INDIVIDUALS AND IDEAS

One of the concerns expressed by some observers of the Paracollege is that students working on their own may become isolated, cut off from the normal social life of the college, or narrowly influenced by one or two tutors. This anxiety (usually the parents'), has proven to be unfounded. Paracollege students live with general college students in the college dormitories, eat in the college cafeteria, and share social and extracurricular activities with the rest of the student body. Any course in the college for which they have the prerequisites is open to them.

But more important, the seminar and tutorial modes of instruction assure that the student will not be able to remain passive, inattentive, or unengaged with his own education. There is no back row in a tutorial; interaction with the material assigned and with the tutor is the essence of the experience. Similarly, the successful seminar exposes the student to the view-points of his fellow students, the seminar leader, and the authors of the texts, or artists, or composers whose work is being studied. In these settings his own ideas are solicited, heard, and refined in conversation with the other participants. The amount of interaction a student has with a faculty member in a single tutor-ial session will exceed that student's interaction with a faculty member during a whole semester in a class of 40 students, unless that student dominates the class's question period, (should the lecturer provide one).

Concern that a student not become isolated in his work, cut off from participation in a community of mind and activity is legitimate. But community is not formed by the proximity of bodies in a classroom. It is formed by mutual commitment to a shared enterprise, whether it be raising a family, producing a play, or reading a text. There is precious little community in most class-rooms because the enterprise is not joined in mutual-ity; rather, students are joined (isolated?) in compet-ition with one another to learn what the teacher has decided is worth their knowing. This decision by the teacher is expected in a course system where the teach-er is responsible for planning and presenting a course; it is justified to the extent she has reflected longer and perhaps more deeply than her students on the topic she proposes for their study. But where the object is to have the students "reflect" upon the subject, re-flect, literally "to be thrown back upon" the subject, she must take care not to subvert that process by filling the hour with her own reflections. She should be aware that in the lecture she will have to work hard to present "diverse individuals and ideas," a process more naturally achieved in an instructional setting where greater responsibility for participation is ex-pected of the students.

LEARNING BY DIRECT AND VARIED EXPERIENCE

Because Paracollege students are not required to complete a specific number of courses for graduation they are free, indeed, are encouraged to explore a variety of ways of learning as they prepare for their comprehensive examinations and senior projects. They may go on field trips appropriate to their tutorial topics. They may be directed into research projects that give them a sense of the reward and difficulty that attends research in the sciences. In most years about ten percent of the Paracollege students participate in study abroad or domestic study programs off campus. They may incorporate their experience with the diverse international studies programs of the college into their educational plans and senior contracts. Students in the general college system must make such experiences equivalent to a standard course; Paracollege students may integrate the experience into their comprehensive examinations, or use the data and experience gathered abroad as the basis for their senior projects.

Since education in the Paracollege is not bound to the course unit, study experiences may vary in duration. The length of a tutorial can be governed by the nature of the material studied, or the availability of material for study. Colloquia can be arranged to meet for a day, or a weekend. Tutorial students or a small seminar can easily travel to lectures, concerts, exhibitions, or hearings that are relevant to the subject being studied. The course unit is a handy measure of hours spent in a classroom, but too restrictive and inflexible a measure of direct and varied experience. One of the things we find it important to remind new students about in the Paracollege is that it is possible to learn a very great deal outside the classroom. Students know this, of course, but they have learned to invalidate the significance of such learning because it has not occurred in a setting defined as "educational." Helping students see the connection between academic subjects (which come from and are about the experience of being human), and their own experiences as human subjects - experiences that counterpoint, illustrate, and become the stuff of new academic subjects - is the aim of such direct and varied experience. What students see, hear, feel, and do outside the classroom, their lives beyond the bounds of the campus, must be engaged by the tutor, informed by texts from the library, and critically appreciated as a part of each student's curriculum.

If one of the aims of liberal arts study is to produce the lifelong learner, then it is important that students acquire the habit of extramural learning and reacquire confidence in the legitimacy of their own questions and in their capacity to frame answers. Lifelong learning does not begin at graduation. It begins at birth, it is devalued in most schools, and is supposed to emerge in full strength and confidence as the last echoes of "Pomp and Circumstance" fade into the mist on graduation day. Is it any wonder that liberal arts graduates ask, "What can I do with my education?" if throughout it all they have felt that they weren't participating in a self-sustaining, life-enhancing process?

Obviously, direct experience in learning can take place inside the lecture hall, seminar, and tutorial as well as outside the classroom. Paracollege instructional methods supplement, but do not replace more traditional ways of teaching. Paracollege students confront their tutors face to face, usually one to one. They are not asked to memorize someone else's integration of ideas (usually the teacher's or that of some other "authority" in the field). They are challenged to think through and articulate their own integration of the topics at hand with the meanings, world view, or aesthetic preferences they bring to that meeting. The author who is read is a third party in the discussion, and must be given the fair reading he deserves just as the student deserves a fair hearing in the tutorial. Direct experience does not mean trial and error for the student, floundering about without direction or resources, a little learning and a lot of fruitless "experimenting;" nor does it discredit the faculty member's hard-won expertise. Rather, a teacher who is alert to the student's need for direct experience will use her expertise to direct the student to those texts, those questions, those experiments which in her professional judgement are most apt to stimulate thought and understanding in the student. Her suggestion of texts to the student is neither prescriptive nor proscribing; "Try this one, I found it helpful in these ways..." rather than, "The answers to your questions are on page 350 of volume II (and that is what I will expect to see on your exam)."

TRANSCENDING THE VIEWPOINT OF AUTHORITIES

One of the aims of a liberal education is to help students develop a context for informed, critical, autonomous judgement. In the Paracollege we discourage students from merely parroting ideas they learned at high school, home, and Sunday school. We teach that the truth of an idea is not derived from the "authority" who affirms it. In William Perry's wonderful study of the intellectual and ethical development of young men at Harvard (Perry 1970), we see the perplexity of young people as they try to figure out who or what constitutes the criteria by which an authority can be regarded as authoritative. The Harvard students, like those at St. Olaf, struggle to discriminate between Authorities whose statements they regard as true because their own family, religion, or peer group has asserted they are, and authority based on available data, logical coherence, or empirical validation. As they struggle to define their authorities - sometimes consciously, sometimes not - some of the students awaken to their own authority as thinking, feeling persons intimately involved in the outcome.

The struggle does not belong to the student alone. Perhaps the hardest developmental task for any teacher is to achieve an appropriate sense of her own authority. Asking in what sense one is an authority brings to intense focus the cognitive self (what I know), and the affective self (how I feel about what I know, how I feel others regard my knowledge, and how I feel about myself as the knower). Insecurity about myself as one who knows can make me defensive when I teach or learn; it can make me intolerant of questions and of those who ask them; or it can be manifest as self-invalidation, a timidity that stills the tongue even as it agitates the stomach. How I feel about what I know can make me an evangelical bigot in the presentation of my knowledge, or, at the other extreme, a well-informed mouse who is so sure no one cares what she knows that she asks herself "Why should I bother sharing it." What we know is complexly related to the variety of experiences we have had and to our more or less tacit epistemological convictions about what is knowable. The permutations of these elements are vast, and some of the variations and their developmental progression are wonderfully presented in Perry's seminal work (1970).

An appropriate sense of authority, as opposed to being Authoritarian, is concomitant with a sense of relative competence in a particular area. Personal authority, in this sense, derives from a realistic assessment of how one has come to know what one does, and, for the teacher, how others may come to know it; it also carries within it awareness of the limits of one's knowledge and experience. Good teachers are comfortable acknowledging what they do not know because they can distinguish what they know from themselves as the knower. Therefore, what they know can be engaged, shared, modified, or changed without eliciting anxiety about who they are or about their personal authority.

The development of a sense of authority grows from the awareness that knowledge does not exist of itself, unchanging, or that it simply appears, like the sun every morning. Personal authority grows as we see how knowledge is produced by human minds in specific times and places, and that we ourselves have such minds and are producers of knowledge. Authorities, the capital "A" variety, speak as if their knowledge were timeless and placeless. Good students agree, and learn to give them little time or place.

Teaching that involves students in the questioning of "answers," and in the construction and defense of their own answers accomplishes two important tasks. It properly relativizes authority, giving it forever a human face, rooting it in a culture, time, and place; and it initiates students into the role of being an authority, owning and presenting ideas as the fruits of their own scholarship and thought. Such teaching pre-supposes a level of maturity in the tutor that enables her comfortably to acknowledge the limits of her own knowledge and methods. (We have all had experience, I suspect, with teachers for whom this was not the case). It also requires that the teacher be confident of the authority her discipline rightfully has, and be able to evaluate and challenge on appropriate grounds the in-adequacies in her students' thought, writing, and re-search. Becoming such a teacher often requires involve-ment in a process of personal and professional develop-ment that parallels the cognitive and affective growth of her student. How the Paracollege innovation promotes such development among its faculty as well as among its students is the theme of the next chapter.

INVOLVEMENT IN EVALUATION AND SELF-ASSESSMENT

Evaluation in the Paracollege is conducted, for the most part, within the context of teaching. Tutors res-pond to students' writing and speaking, to their propo-sals and ideas as they are presented. In a tutorial, for example, there is no need for a formal quiz over that week's assignment. From the student's prepared responses to the week's reading, and from his sponta-neous questions and responses to inquiry from the tutor it is apparent what he has understood, what is muddled in his mind, and what has been missed altogether. Evaluation is not inserted at midterm or tacked on at the end of a course; it is inherent in the dialogue between tutor and student.

Further, since the student has been instrumental in defining the area of his study and the subject of his tutorial he is in a position to assess whether his questions are being answered and if his efforts are proving fruitful, or whether some wider or narrower definition of his subject might bring him closer to his goal. The tutor's query, "Is this approach helpful to you?" invites self-assessment as well as evaluation of the tutor's contribution to the tutorial. Since the student is not being graded on his work in the tutorial, the tutor's corrections and suggestions are not a summative judgement marking the end of a learning experience, recalled as a success if "I got an A," or a failure if "I got a D." Rather, the week to week comments of tutors become guides for the next week's work; students question tutors, seeking more specific evaluation of their work; evaluations become integral parts of the instructional process itself. At the end of a unit of study the tutor writes a narrative report of the work accomplished by the student, describing its strengths and weaknesses, and summarises what has been their ongoing experience, citing remarkable accomplishments, if there have been some, as well as areas in which additional work could be profitably undertaken.

FREEING ONESELF FROM EXCESSIVE ANXIETY

A college must present a student with tasks that challenge and enlarge her repetoire of skills and understanding. If it does not, she is wasting her money there. Rising to the challenge is one way to speak of development in college. Everyone is not equal to every challenge, but neither do all challenges foster development. Some challenges evoke such high levels of anxiety that learning is not the result, but, instead, intellectual paralysis, insomnia, illness, and varieties of avoidance behavior, some chemically abetted. Nor is anxiety in the face of overwhelming challenge a response peculiar to students. (Do not most faculty reading this know something of writer's block, for example?) Anxiety is a normal response to challenge. What is educationally, developmentally important is to help students learn how to respond to challenges, how to raise their "whelming level" when they begin to find the challenges too great.

The best model I have found that explains this phenomenon generally and that is specifically relevant to the Paracollege as a setting for student development is Richard Jones' model of learning:

A MODEL OF LEARNING

IMAGINATION + ALONE + HELPLESSNES = ANXIETY ← PSYCHOTHERAPY

TEACHING → IMAGINATION + COMMUNITY + MASTERY = CREATIVE LEARNING

(Richard Jones, 1968, p.77)

According to Jones, in therapy the point of contact with the client is the client's anxiety. The client enlists the therapist as an ally (community) against his overwhelming ideas, images, and feelings. By his presence and interpretation of the clients' confusion the therapist helps transform what had been a sense of helplessness into a sense of mastery.

The teacher differs from the therapist in that her point of contact with the student is not the student's anxiety but the student's imagination. The commerce of education is ideas, and the teacher's proper task is the stimulation of the student's ideas. But the stimulation of the imagination without the concurrent experience of community that leads to mastery results in anxiety, not learning. Which of us has not had the experience of watching a teacher unscroll a math problem across the blackboard, the terms of which were opaque to us, and felt the rising tide of tension from our solar plexus? Completely in the dark, not knowing where to turn for help without violating the admonition, 'Do your own work,' we struggled with the feelings of failure, humiliation, embarrassment, and self-loathing which themselves inhibited effective problem-solving. Or, which of us has not found ourselves staring in dumb-struck unrecognition in a foreign language class at an irregular verb form to be conjugated, palms sweaty, eyes darting here and there looking for an exit? We were challenged, all right, but were helpless to meet what was more of an assault than a challenge to our abilities. Despairing of learning, we alternately damned the language, the teacher, and our ignorance for conspiring to bring us to such a fate. A teacher is successful to the degree she can establish community with the anxious student. She may do this by her own presence or by evoking a sense of community within the

45

class. The point is to not abandon the student to his anxiety, but to enable him to move from bewildered helplessness to mastery of the images that have challenged his understanding.

A teacher who does not challenge the imagination does not teach; but neither does one who by her challenges intimidates and isolates her students. Her students may find one another after class, banding together for mutual support, encouragement, and understanding, thereby establishing community and moving toward insight despite the teacher (the Paper Chase syndrome). Or self-reliant students may find the support of community in the text, or reference books in the library, if they are the independent sort who know where to look for help. But the best teachers are not those whose students succeed in spite of them, but those who so construct their lectures, so direct their seminars, or so conduct tutorials that students experience the teacher as a partner in the learning enterprise. Good teachers demonstrate how they, themselves, find community with others in the face of challenging ideas, problems, and questions. These "others" may be colleagues, librarians, or students, or allies in the form of reference books or search strategies. Such teachers have given thought to how it is they learn, where they find their own intellectual stimulation, and how they manage their own anxiety in the face of an intellectual challenge. They allow their students to know the sequences of their minds as well as the consequences of their study.

The structure of Paracollege pedagogy induces much anxiety in its students. (It does so in its faculty as well, as we shall see later.) The thought of sitting face to face with a college professor for an hour a week daunts most eighteen year olds. The knowledge that to graduate they must devise a subject concentration, write comprehensive exams, undergo an oral examination in their field, and produce a senior project that demonstrates their competence in their field of study is a challenge which, frankly, turns many prospective Paracollegians back to the familiar routines of taking notes, writing term papers, and taking exams in every course. These are familiar challenges, hurdles they have already proven proficient in surmounting.

Students rise to the challenges presented by the Paracollege because its modes of instruction maximize their opportunities to regulate their anxiety levels. The anxiety that precedes tutorial experience is miti-

46

gated by the presence of a tutor who is "on their side" in their quest for knowledge, and who soon learns "where they are" in their understanding of a topic. Students quickly find out that their questions, their confusions about the material assigned that week are the best bases for discussion. The student's tutorial is not an exercise in trying to hide what he does not know, but is an opportunity to refine his understanding and extend his knowledge beyond its current base. The student's admission, "I don't understand," is not the occasion for having his grade lowered but the point at which pertinent discussion can begin.

Tutors report that one of the great satisfactions in their role is the rediscovery of what it is like to be an undergraduate. How little or how much each student knows, and how slowly or rapidly each student can learn the material becomes apparent. The tutor can adjust the degree of challenge in his assignments, can assess the point where the student's necessary struggle for mastery verges on floundering, pointless bewilderment, or outright avoidance. Tutors can perceive when each student needs more information, or more encouragement, or a more powerfully integrating theory to organize the information with which they are struggling. Teaching becomes a genuinely interpersonal dialogue, a humanizing experience for students and faculty alike.

ACHIEVING MEANINGFUL GOALS

"What an organism does, as William Perry says, is organize (1970); and what a human organism organizes is meaning." (Kegan p.11, 1982). How many hours of how many campus counsellors' days are spent listening to the student complaint, "I just don't see anything meaningful in my studies. I don't see any point in what I'm doing. None of the courses I'm taking interests me, but they are required for graduation"? How many dormitory bull sessions revolve around the same themes: damn assignments, damn requirements, damn routines? If Victor Frankl is right, and the making of meaning is the fundamental human motivation; and if Robert Kegan is right, and the making of meaning is the way by which the human organism develops, then students' complaints of the meaninglessness of their lives reflect something profoundly amiss in college education as it is usually pursued.

The coherence of the Paracollege educational process is inherent in the way each student connects its various components. This is a coherence that is not apparent to the outsider; this is why those who believe the power of a curriculum is found in sequences of courses and required "experiences" of breadth are mystified and scandalized by the Paracollege innovation. They have not tumbled to the implications of the fact that experience can never be required or taught. Experience is created within each individual; it is produced by the mind's action upon the data it receives. This is why two students hearing the same lecture will report it as quite different experiences. Requiring a diversity of courses no more guarantees a coherent education than requiring a tour of Europe guarantees intercultural understanding. It is the student's task to integrate her education, to make its meanings full. Memorizing someone else's integration is not a "meaning-full" experience.

Because the Paracollege requires each person to organize his and her own meaning, Paracollege students must answer the question "Why?" as well as "What?" when they propose their course of study. This is why all freshmen must devise a plan for their general education that states how the course of study they propose is appropriate in its breadth (meets the college's general education requirement) and, at the same time, is appropriate for them specifically (is meaningfully related to their current understanding and aspirations). This is why all seniors must describe how their studies cohere in a meaningful way and comprise a concentration with scope suitable for a baccalaureate degree. The principle of coherence, of integration, is within each student; it develops from and with them as they work the broad requirements of the college into individually meaningful programs of study.

Whatever complaints Paracollege students share with other college students, meaninglessness in their work is not one of them. Ninety-nine percent of the Paracollege students surveyed in 1981 stated that they found their work in the Paracollege more meaningful than work they had done in the general college. Ninety-eight percent agreed that their involvement in the Paracollege was worth the time and effort they put into it. Ninety-six percent found there was concern for them as individuals in the Paracollege, and ninety-four percent found study in the Paracollege fit their academic interests and style. More specific reasons for the high satisfaction reported are detailed in chapter seven. Let us simply note here that the educational process made possible by the Paracollege innovation enables students to achieve goals meaningful to them, both while they are in the midst of the program, and when as alumni they reflect upon their education. Such meaningful study is evidence of that involvement that is the corner-stone of excellence in a learning environment.

CHAPTER FOUR

FACULTY DEVELOPMENT IN THE PARACOLLEGE

As Heiss (1970) has demonstrated in her survey of graduate education, the socializing forces of graduate training are powerful. They can become dehumanizing, when the advancement of the profession comes to be accepted as the paramount good. Faculty members must evolve complex cognitive schemata that take into account the relativity of the norms and values of faculty culture and that reflect their unique adaptation to it and their personal ordering of priorities. This development entails the faculty member's realization that professional roles and conventions are a subset of many possible identities. Faculty members therefore face the existential burden of defining themselves and of finding ways to sustain those definitions.

    Freedman, et al., Academic Culture and Faculty Development, 1979, p. 166

I've always had a tendency to prefer an interdisciplinary learning approach, but my graduate training was specifically a strict experimental training program. The Paracollege has allowed me to regain some of the breadth which was limited during that training. However, I'm torn between the two. I am very convinced that the method in which I was trained is the more rigorous, but somehow all that rigor excludes the human qualities. I feel a little like Maslow must have felt when he began to question his training in animal behavior in favor of humanism.

    Social Scientist, Second year in Paracollege

I came to my interest in faculty development through the back door. I had been working as a campus pastor to students before I went to Berkeley to pursue graduate study. Faculty, students had been telling me, were a large part of what was wrong with life at college. Faculty were boring in class, insensitive to what was happening in students' lives, inaccessible when they were needed, and uninterested when students did manage to trap them in their offices. One of the things that happens to students at college is faculty, and in

51

the sixties, it seemed, not much was happening in student-faculty relations.

While at The Wright Institute in Berkeley, interviewing faculty members about their experience with students, I heard an echo of the students' complaints. When I asked faculty to share their perceptions of students and to describe their relationship with them a frequent response was, Do you mean graduate or undergraduate students? Clearly, students were one of the things that happened to faculty, but the level of the student determined what was happening as far as faculty were concerned. For many faculty, undergraduates were to colleges what flies are to picnics. If there was pleasure or stimulation to be found in teaching, it lay in work with graduate students.

These generalizations, however, did not apply to all students, nor to all faculty. Here and there I would interview a student or a faculty member who found stimulation and not merely provocation in the teaching relationship. The diversity in student-faculty relations became clear while I was studying faculty's lives and experience at the Center for Research and Development in Higher Education in Berkeley. I interviewed faculty on several campuses who had been nominated by their peers and students as outstanding teachers. These faculty were not asleep at their lecterns nor were they hiding from their undergraduate students. Some of these faculty were young, in the first decade of their career. Others were in mid-career, while still others were near retirement, bearing scars of years of academic campaigning, though neither halt, lame, nor nursing their wounds. The task of the Center's research was to identify factors in the academic setting that enabled and supported good teaching, and we asked questions designed to elicit such information. Our research for The Wright Institute, on the other hand, had a more personal focus. There we asked faculty questions that probed what it was like to be a teacher at that particular campus, what the frustrations were, where and when they found satisfaction in their work, what they valued in students, what they tried to achieve in the classroom, and what visions and hopes they had for their careers. These studies provided a rich sense of how different teaching environments, "academic cultures" we called them, could enable or constrain the personal and professional development of faculty on different campuses.

One of the notable findings of these studies was

that the kinds of relationships faculty had with students, whether graduate or undergraduate students, were a salient factor in the academic culture. Upon reflection it does not seem all that surprising that those relationships with faculty that students found most educational were the same kinds of relationships that the faculty found most stimulating. Students wanted to be known as the persons they were, to have their questions listened to and responded to seriously. They wanted faculty to acknowledge that they had lives and experiences and agendas that were not coterminous with the classroom. They were stimulated by faculty who shared their research problems and questions with them. They knew when they were being challenged by one of Jefferson's American Scholars, "a man thinking," and when they were being fed warmed up lecture notes. They felt cheated by faculty who were entertaining but intellectually insubstantial, who assumed authority because of the side of the desk they occupied, and who presumed that little worth hearing, much less knowing, resided in the nameless crania arrayed in ranks before them. Good teachers were organized, personal, accessible, demanding, and fair. It helped if they had a sense of humor, but sarcasm and muchupsmanship won neither respect nor admiration.

The part played by each faculty member in the relationship varied depending on the extent to which each had integrated his personal values and identity with his professional role as a member of a discipline and with the values of his particular institution. Most faculty valued students who were intellectually involved (committed, if they were graduate students), whose questions were serious if not always insightful, and who respected them for what they knew but who were more than dutiful note-takers bringing "their sheep faces to Tuesday"(John Ciardi). What they objected to in undergraduate teaching, when they did object, was the "low level" at which they had to teach, and the passive students who took whatever they dished out. These students were as much scorned as were students who made no pretence of interest in their subject whatever; indeed, both are variations of the same disengaged student.

It became apparent that what students needed and desired, if they were to develop as students, were teachers who were themselves engaged in the process of developing. As in any interpersonal encounter in which thought, emotion, effort, and value are invested, it is the quality of interaction and not merely the maintenance of the form that is enlivening. Of course the setting in which the interaction takes place can seriously limit or broadly support opportunities for stimulating interaction. Some institutions seem designed to keep faculty and students from talking together; others reward faculty who teach brilliantly despite institutional constraints against teaching. Some few colleges develop an academic culture where vital exchange is the norm and where deviation from that norm means empty classrooms, no tenure, and no promotion for the faculty.

THE PARACOLLEGE

The Paracollege provides an institutional setting that supports personal and professional development of faculty who work within it. Indeed, one reason it has such powerful impact on students is because it has impact upon faculty as well. Insight as to why this is so can be found in Nevitt Sanford's book, Learning After College (1980), in which he presents nine general propositions that are relevant to adult development in general and to faculty development in particular:

NINE PROPOSITIONS CONCERNING ADULT DEVELOPMENT

1. For a change in personality to occur there must be a change in behavior.
2. A change of behavior depends upon the presence of an appropriate and effective challenge, one that is sufficient to upset equilibrium but not so extreme as to induce regression by surpassing the limits of the adaptive capacities we call ego strength.
3. In childhood and adolescence there are usually challenges in abundance but adults will ordinarily require a change in general situation - in the social roles, relationships, responsibilities, and reward system systems that structure life and are, in effect, external barriers to development.
4. Personality development requires the knowledge, or at least the implicit assumption, that one can develop.
5. Freedom from external barriers to change, and the knowledge that change is possible, have to be supplemented by positive stimuli to action in order for significant change in behavior to occur.
6. A challenge must be experienced as such, and it must be accepted, if it is to induce durable change in behavior.

7. Steps can be taken to prevent the projection onto new situations of psychological contents from the past, to overcome resistance to the assimilation of knowledge, to assist alternative ways of behaving, and to connect new stimuli with inner needs and potentialities.
8. Personality development in adults requires self-examination aimed at self-insight.
9. People develop together.

Sanford, (1980), pp 61-66.

While Sanford's schema for adult development is applicable to a variety of settings, I find its force and rationality are admirably demonstrated in the Paracollege. In the rest of this chapter we will look at Sanford's propositions for adult development as they relate specifically to Paracollege faculty development.

CHANGE IN BEHAVIOR

The developmental rationale for "breadth requirements" for undergraduates is that by testing their intellect, emotions, and bodies in diverse situations with various subjects, students will acquire a realistic sense of their interests and competencies. It is hoped they will retain from these studies enough knowledge to provide a sophisticated context for weighing decisions they must make during their lifetime. A course of study that offers no challenges to students' patterns of thinking, feeling, and acting is devoid of developmental significance. This is why some really bright students can float through a course of study and remain largely unaffected by it; they simply use the skills they acquired in a good secondary education to make the necessary grades, but are not required to behave in ways that are essentially new to them.

What can happen to good students can happen to good faculty as well, especially in an institution whose challenges and reward structures encourage the repetition of skills acquired in graduate school, and little else. Faculty are presumed to have met their "breadth requirements" when they were undergraduates, but as Heiss (1970) discovered, the pressures of graduate school can reduce one's scope of self-definition even as they refine one's professional skills. Further, we know that information that lay dead on the page for us when we were eighteen years old can rivet our attention when twenty years of additional living have given us a context for understanding and assimilating it. Faculty report that teaching in the Paracollege has been a recovery, and for some the acquisition, of their own liberal education. They have had to behave differently in the Paracollege. They have had to work closely with a subset of the whole college's faculty; they team-teach seminars they helped design with colleagues from other disciplines. The reward from teaching in the Paracollege most often mentioned by its faculty is the experience of working with colleagues from other disciplines, and the consequent broadening of the perspectives they had acquired in graduate school.

I do not mean to denigrate the perspectives and skills acquired in graduate training. They are essential to the work of scholarship in the disciplines. Newly minted Ph.D.'s, having spent the most recent years of their life in focused study, are valued precisely because of their closeness to the leading edge of scholarship and their idealism about what can be done in the profession. "New blood," we call them. But it isn't their platelets that make them valuable to an institution; it is their new ways of behaving, their new questions; they are the occasion for us to rethink why it is we have been behaving as we have in the department or the division.

The opportunity to bring new people into our old settings is strictly limited, however, by the number of faculty positions allocated to a department or division. Another way to change behavior is to place older faculty in new positions, where they may draw upon the knowledge and skills they have acquired but must use those skills to present that knowledge in ways that reorganize their accustomed ways of teaching. As Neugarten's studies of adults development have shown, old dogs can learn new tricks, especially if they are intelligent old dogs to begin with (Neugarten, 1968).

Faculty who work in the Paracollege are required to change their behavior in significant ways. Relinquishing total control of the teaching hour is one such change, and many faculty report difficulty in doing this in tutorials. Most of our experience as teachers has been that we do much while the students do little. We haven't minded; we like to study. We tell our colleagues, gratified to our depths, that we have managed to find five hours for uninterrupted study. We long for sabbatical leave when we can find those uninterrupted hours every day. However, we admit to one another that we really came to know our material when we had to teach it.

In tutorials, on the other hand, we learn how to teach more by doing less; talking less, probably, but listening more, which to an onlooker might appear to be doing less but to the student usually feels like more. Students find that they, like we, really come to know a subject when they have to explain it to someone. But they rarely have the chance because faculty are behaving in the ways we have observed and learned best; we talk while students listen. We devote study to primary and secondary texts and discuss in our lectures the background and implications of material, while students read the text book and prepare a term paper. No wonder we learn and retain it better than our students do! In tutorials the faculty learn the truth of Ortega y Gasset's dictum, "Scarcity of the capacity to learn is the cardinal principle of education. It is necessary to provide for teaching precisely in proportion as the learner is unable to learn." (Ortega, quoted in Becker, 1967 p.55).

One seasoned Paracollege tutor, drawing on his Norwegian ethnic heritage, says that tutorials are like trolls. You never know what they are going to be like until you meet them. They are always different, each one unique, some dreadful, some funny, some very helpful. In every case, however, if you are going to be successful, you have to be at the top of your form, alert, not fooled or lulled or distracted, but responsive. The good tutor is one who understands and behaves as Buber says a teacher must, listening and responding to the person who is present, not to the abstract "student," who is seated as a case in point across from you.

UPSET EQUILIBRIUM

Some faculty find the challenge of meeting with an undergraduate for an hour at a time too unsettling. They may feel they are wasting time they could better use in a classroom with forty students. Certainly they are more comfortable in that familiar setting. Others find they cannot relinquish control of the hour; dialogue on the topic of the day, asking the student questions, seeking clarification, and providing answers to the student's real questions about the material are not sufficiently gratifying for some faculty. Working on an interdisciplinary class, or team-teaching, may tax the faculty members' powers of adaptation to a degree they find uncomfortable. Growth may entail discomfort, a truism with which we console our complaining students, but one we are reluctant to accept in our own case. In fact, two-thirds of the faculty working in the Paracollege report that they entered into the work with some anxiety, an indication that they found the work to be psychologically challenging.

Data from an earlier survey of faculty in the Paracollege in the 1970's show that some faculty reported it was a negative experience for them. These faculty, however, had been in the Paracollege two years or less. Was the challenge too great, or was the support provided these faculty inadequate to assist them through the changes in behavior required by the Paracollege? The histories of the early years in most educational innovations include reports of high levels of stress induced by marathon faculty meetings, fuzzy expectations about what success in the work might look like, and uncertainty as to whether the sponsoring institution would validate and reward the faculty's efforts. This is certainly a "challenge...sufficient to upset equilibrium." It may also have been "extreme ...surpassing the limits of adaptive capacities" for some faculty. Discussions with the founding members of the Paracollege faculty indicate that considerable stress attended the early years of the innovation, which may well account for the disenchantment of some of their colleagues.

PLANNING FOR CHANGE IN THE LIFE STRUCTURE SYSTEM

If changes in behavior are prerequisite to personal development and these changes are sparked in adult life by an alteration in one's general situation - one's roles, relationships, or responsibilities - then it would be wise for faculty to plan episodes in their careers when they will be challenged to restructure, adapt, and reorder their patterns of behavior. Some faculty we interviewed in the Wright Institute studies testified to their need for new challenges. Usually these were faculty who had been successful according to the values foremost on their particular campus. It is as if they had met the challenges in their particular setting and dreaded continuing endlessly in a routine that they knew well and that had no mysterious horizon. Sometimes they were angling for positions at other campuses. Sometimes they felt the uncertain call to become administrators. Sometimes, dug into the domestic trenches of family, spouse's work and children's schools, with no realistic prospects of leaving their institution, they looked to avocations for stimulation. Others, particularly at prestigious institutions, un-

able to climb higher and hemmed in by departmental constraints, seemed resigned to continue what they had
been doing, hoping that NEH or NSF might give them a
ladder over the wall for a sanctioned escape.

A program like the Paracollege provides a setting
within the institution where faculty may expand their
repertoires of teaching skills, where they can engage
in the investigation and discussion of interesting
problems with colleagues from other disciplines, and in
which they can develop ideas outside the area of their
regular teaching assignments. For some faculty this has
been the opportunity to return to a much-loved topic
that had been pursued in graduate school, but which
they had not been asked to teach in their department.
Others have found colleagues from other departments who
shared their interests; together they have offered
seminars that were enriching to them and stimulating to
students. "Democracy and the Public Interest" linked
the research of faculty in economics and political
science. "Creativity" was the theme of a seminar led by
faculty in psychology and creative writing. "America on
Stage" was the vehicle through which an American
historian and a professor of English examined the movement for social change in the 1920's and 1930's through
the dramas written in that period.

The point is, institutions can provide settings for
teaching that encourage and reward faculty for behaving
in ways not usually possible in the standard classroom.
Faculty need not leave their campus, their other teaching duties, or their departments. Colleges need not
expend large sums of money to provide such alternative
settings; and, as we have seen, students no less than
faculty can benefit by such changes.

The Paracollege meets Sanford's third requirement
for adult development. It changes the general situation
within which faculty work. Their social roles vis a vis
colleagues and students are altered. They continue to
be responsible for teaching, curriculum, and evaluation, but in order to discharge these responsibilities
they must rethink and reorganize many of their accustomed ways of behaving. Rewards are found in these
modes of teaching, but they are largely those of personal satisfaction, vocational fulfillment, and direct
encounter with students who are eager to learn, and
with colleagues who share the burden and excitement of
meaningful work. One tutor in physics put it this way,
"It allows me to integrate scientific knowledge and
skills in a number of areas of everyday life and to do

this as a legitimate part of my work. Thus within the definition of my 'job' I am able to function as a more whole person. I do not have to separate one part of my life from another".

CHANGE IS POSSIBLE

The work of Jung, and more lately that of Levinson (1978), Sheehy (1976), and Gould (1978), has instructed the larger population about the possibilities for adult development. Teachers need not think themselves exceptions to these general findings. Change is possible. One is not fated to repeat the same routines year after year. There are colleagues whose attitudes transcend jealousy, defensiveness, and competition. One may feel as vital and productive at fifty-five as at twenty-five. Such beliefs are important to adult development. They argue against those inner voices that counsel acceptance of compromise of the ideals that brought many of us into teaching. Indeed, some faculty are aware of how great a distance they have come from the hesitant enthusiasm of their first appointment to the richly textured thought and feeling they have acquired through years in their profession. As one of the Paracollege tutors put it, "I've been able to do student-centered learning, with myself as one of the students, so I've been able to pose lots of questions I've had. Even more broadly though, I've been able to be an educator (leading students out) more than a teacher (filling students up). When I started in the Paracollege, I wanted to cover material for my students, and uncover new data for the professional community of historians. Now I want to uncover ideas for students, broadcast them to a broader community, and let the historians fend for themselves. I'm more interested in synthesis and coherence, both educationally and professionally, than before." In fairness to this particular tutor, the transformation of his educational philosophy and professional aims has not been to the detriment of the community of historians. He has published two books during his six years in the Paracollege and has presented his work regularly at professional meetings.

One of the motivations for the founding of cluster colleges in the sixties was the hope that they would provide impetus for change within their large sponsoring institutions. It was hoped they could be models that demonstrated to the larger institution new ways of organizing curriculum and new ways of making faculty resources available to students outside the standard departmental structure. In some instances, where the cluster model was not too much at variance with the dominant academic culture on campus, many salutary changes were brought about through the influence of the innovating cluster college. At St. Olaf College there was hope the Paracollege would be a kind of "tug boat" exerting continuing pressure to move the larger institution in some new directions. I will discuss in chapters five and six how the Paracollege has been both a model and an impetus to change; what I want to note in this context is that faculty have perceived in the Paracollege a setting in which change can and does occur in faculty as well as in students. It is not the only setting "where the action is" by any means. But its programs and faculty do provide a continuing reminder that there is more than one way to play the academic game, and that players of every age can extend their scope and versatility as teachers within it. I take it as a healthy sign that faculty inquire about how they might become involved with the Paracollege. It indicates that faculty do not perceive a stint of teaching in the Paracollege as the equivalent of the students' "required course," but as a valued resource for their own development in the college.

STIMULI TO ACTION

Positive stimuli for faculty to change take several forms in the Paracollege. First, there is the presence of colleagues whose interest in teaching and whose discussions of educational practice and philosophy add an ingredient to the academic culture that may be lacking in the more settled and traditional department. Academic culture does not permit faculty to publicly disavow interest in teaching. Most faculty, however, have had little time or inclination to think about themselves in their roles as teachers. It is not what graduate schools trained them to do. But when they find themselves to be part of a faculty for whom the rationale for what is taught and the most effective methods for teaching it are scrutinized and debated, what often has been their latent, presumed, but undeveloped pedagogical philosophy is brought to conscious, critical awareness. This shared reflection on the common work of teaching is an impetus to change. As one tutor put it, "It (the Paracollege) hasn't made me change my vocation, but the reflection that comes from Paracollege faculty and policy have given me much better reasons (and better ways) for doing what I thought I was doing before." Another tutor with fewer years in the Paracollege observed, " I expected it to accelerate and give more accurate direction to changes that had already begun in me. And that it is doing."

There have been some small material incentives for
faculty to rethink their teaching philosophy and
behavior. The Paracollege has sought and received
grants that faculty have used to assess the effectiveness of their work in the Paracollege. In addition,
faculty have received money from the college's faculty
development funds to help finance meetings during summer months to devise new curricula for the general
education program of the Paracollege. Some of this work
is discussed in chapter five. The funds allotted were
not large, but they have constituted an important endorsement by the college, a material investment in
pedagogical values that too frequently are given only
lip service. Further, such small grants have permitted
faculty to purchase materials and to maintain discussion of alternative teaching methods during the summer
months.

ACCEPTING THE CHALLENGE

Academic culture is, paradoxically, aggressively
conservative. Innovative concepts must always prove
their worth in the face of entrenched scepticism. Participation in educational experiments by those who
initiate them, and by those who are new to the sponsoring institution or new to their professions, can generally be regarded as professionally hazardous. Faculty
who champion the cause of innovation should understand
that by doing so they challenge the methods and at
times the values that undergird the time-honored teaching practices and behavior of their colleagues. These
methods and values are knit into the fabric of academic
culture. The failed endeavors of every decade testify
to the power of academic tradition to stifle innovative
ideas about how education might proceed. That the innovation succumbed no more argues against its educational value than the duck is proved an inefficient
flyer by the shot-gun that picks him out of the morning
sky. The inequalities of power are just too great.

The faculty's perception that work in the Paracollege can be a valuable experience for them is one of
the most important factors in its success. Faculty,
like most people anywhere, want to know what benefit
may accrue to them from their effort, especially if the
effort is outside the bounds of what is usually expected on their campus. Further, if the benefits are uncertain, it must be absolutely clear that there are no
penalties accruing for faculty who participate in the

innovation. If a department regards working in the
innovation as professionally suspect it is understand-
able that tutors from that department would be tentative about venturing into it.

What is significant about the Paracollege in this
context is not merely that it has persisted for eighteen years. That is significant. But more important,
during that passage of years a large number of faculty
has experienced the challenge and the rewards of the
enterprise. The Paracollege has had time to become the
faculty's program in fact as well as word. That faculty
seek to be a part of it testifies to its acceptance
within the academic culture; it is seen to provide
opportunities for their own development.

MEETING INNER NEEDS

My purpose is not to compare the experiences of
faculty inside with those of faculty outside the Paracollege. It is, rather, to identify those characteristics of the innovation that have had developmental
significance for the faculty who work within it. It is
these faculty who, seeing the challenge, have also seen
the possibilities for themselves and have taken them up
with interest and devotion. One faculty member describes his needs and how they were met in the
Paracollege:

I had become used to teaching large classes, with the intention of moving them through
a large body of material. I was used to carrying the main burden of the class, by lectur-
ing or at least leading discussion. Intellectually I was becoming increasingly suspicious
of what I would call the mechanization of
thinking and writing within my field
(literature), and the way in which the discipline was subject to the passing vagaries of
critical fashion, not to mention the spirit-
shriveling effects of ever narrower specialization (for the sake of "professionalism").
The emphasis in the Paracollege on interdisciplinary work has strengthened my confidence in the breadth and interconnectedness of
knowledge. It has provided me with the chance
to cultivate a much more intimate teaching
style. It has eased the burden (that in regular courses it is so easy to convince oneself
it is necessary to carry) of trying to
cover everything in a sequence of study: meet-

ing once a week in a tutorial compels me to distinguish the essential from the incidental. I am far less concerned with saying everything completely than with saying a few things memorably.

This talented member of the faculty is known for his ability to lecture brilliantly. It is significant that he is not content to remain within his demonstrated strength but has been eager to try his skill on new ground. He continues, "The rewards I know...are those of tutorial teaching - personal attention to the particular and unique needs and intelligence of individual students, with all the obvious advantages of being able to help a student forward with a swiftness and accuracy unknown in the setting of the larger class. More particularly, there is the reward of extended intellectual argument and discussion." This colleague is not blind to the weaknesses of the program, nor to the anxiety it engenders in his fellow tutors; "The Paracollege is a living challenge to maintain intellectual breadth and generosity, with the concomitant moral and emotional attributes. The camaraderie of the Paracollege can be rather phoney, the good humor more the result of nervous anxiety in the presence of colleagues only just this side of being strangers rather than of easy familiarity." He here acknowledges the reality of the challenge and of some colleagues' not-always-appreciated methods of coping with it. He goes on to say, "But despite this, the Paracollege mixes us up with each other, across disciplines, divisions and departments, in a way that is bracing and healthy. Departments can close minds, the Paracollege can open them."

SELF-INSIGHT.

"I've really come to the conclusion that I'm more interested in my discipline for its teaching value than for its intrinsic value (whatever that is). I enjoy being a 'generic' social scientist."
Political Science tutor

"Students are no longer 'them' but 'us,' part of a community of inquiry."
History tutor

Gaining self-insight is the task of a lifetime, one we hope is stimulated by the liberal arts we teach, but a task no college can guarantee its students will accomplish. We design curricula whose purpose is to foster self-insight. However, the purpose of the most carefully wrought design can fail. No one, young or old, can gain self-insight without **wanting** to do so, and then, as dynamic psychologies have demonstrated, often only with great effort. This being the case, I would still maintain that there are some forms of teaching that are more facilitative of such insight than others.

The tutorial, with its on-going discussion and evaluation of the student's progress is a form that I find produces self-insight. In their dialogue from week to week both tutor and student may hear what each has done that has been helpful to their tutorial session. There is no confusion of tutor's and student's role here; the student does not look for a pal in the tutor, and the tutor has maintained the integrity and self-respect appropriate for one whose greater age and experience in the field may give some additional weight to his comments and counsel. But having said this, the tutorial has provided during the term at least fourteen hours of face to face encounter concerning issues about which both of them genuinely care. What occurs in the evaluation is conducive to insight in both student and tutor.

For example, students tell me what I do in a tutorial that is helpful to them and what is not. They can be frank about where our interests meet or diverge. I learn a great deal about myself from their comments on how I have assessed their work. I find I often presume an interest or an understanding they do not share. I find, at times, that when I think I have spoken clearly the student has found my comments confusing. Or when I feel I have been gentle in my criticism, they have found me to be harsh. How strange it is sometimes to meet myself through the eyes and thoughts of my students! And, face to face with them, how difficult to avoid reflecting on that self that I meet through them.

My comments to them should be no less evocative of their self-insight. Comments made in tutorial are of a different kind than I can give when grading a batch of fifty midterm exams, or term papers. What I scrawl on those papers is easily divorced from its implications for me as a teacher and a person; the student to whom I am writing is not present to respond; although I am conscientious in my comments I am not immediately accountable as the student reads them. What is so for me as the teacher is no less so for the student who riffles through his blue book to discover the summative judgement "B+," and who with an expletive or a sigh of relief casts the exam into the cardboard box containing the relics of his academic past. Teaching evaluation forms, when used during as well as at the end of a course, can provide some potentially helpful but anonymous feedback. (I find your lectures hard to understand? Who is this "I"? Wherein is the difficulty? Is it my vocabulary? grammar? accent? Is it the student's country of origin? Her background in the subject? Her study habits? While I think such teaching evaluations can be of use, they are poor approximations of the kind of rich, specific, thought-provoking comments I am left to ponder at the end of each tutorial. Since the student in the tutorial is not given a letter grade, but a narrative evaluation the contents of which should be no surprise when she reads it, she has much to gain by participating, week to week, in the assessment of the tutorial.

DEVELOP TOGETHER

Sanford's last principle reasserts what has been found to be true in such interrelationships as psychotherapy, parenting, friendships, marriages, and teaching. It is no coincidence that in each of these human relationships only two or just a few more people interact. We are most apt to reflect upon those ideas and activities we value highly, or about which we feel strongly, when we are in relationships with people we trust, our spouses, closest friends, parents, respected teachers, or counselors. We do not ordinarily disclose ourselves to people whom we know only in their social roles. Those of us who are parents know that the years of child raising have changed us. (It's not just as some wag has put it; insanity is hereditary, parents get it from their kids.) The mutuality of interaction that is essential to successful parenting has required us to become more thoughtful, more discriminating in our understanding of others and of ourselves.

The experience of student and faculty as they interrelate in the Paracollege supports John Seely's thesis that good teaching is an extension of the activities that characterize good parenting (See his essay, "The University as Slaughterhouse," Great Ideas Today, 1969). This is not to say that faculty members act in loco parentis, or that they should. It is a recognition that the roles of student and teacher, like those of parent and child, are mutually constituted. The parents' hopes that their children will become healthy, productive, ethically sensitive adults is extended in the teachers' concern that each student will come to understand himself as the unique person he is, with specific competencies and commensurate responsibilities.

What gives higher education its liberating power is not its emphasis upon more abstract conceptual learning, but its perspective that each person is a distinct participant in life who shapes and is shaped by the cultural, spiritual, and intellectual forces of his society. To "know yourself" is to know that you are both a creature and a creator in an expanding network of human relationships that began at birth with your family but that extends backwards in time and forward in hope to some vision of meaningful community on planet Earth. As Seely points out, good teaching is a specific expression of that general concern for human succession that Erikson calls "generativity" (Erikson, 1950). As such it is, or can be for both students and faculty, an opportunity for the mutual experience of intellectual and emotional expansion and delight, discovery, evocation and confirmation of the very persons student and teacher are. That this experience is so infrequent in teaching is one of the tragedies of our traditional educational system.

CHAPTER FIVE

CURRICULUM IN THE PARACOLLEGE

Curricle___Two-wheeled carriage. XVIII-L. curriculum, racing chariot, dim. F. _currere_ (see
prec). In the original sense of 'course' the
L. word curriculum has been adopted (XIX) for
'course of study or training' (orig. in Sc.
universities).
The _Oxford_ _Dictionary_ _of_ _English_ _Etymology_,
1985, p. 237.

Curriculum___<>i.n. (curro + culum) Gender =
curriculus (masc.)... 1. The   action of
running; esp.<>o at the double at a run... 2.
(Transf.) A course of action,a way of behaving.
3. A race; also, a place in the running...b. a
single circuit of a race-track, a lap;...c.
(Fig.) the race of life; also its' laps. 4. A
race track b.(Fig.) a field for the display of
talents. 5. A chariot; esp. for racing.
The _Oxford_ _Latin_ _Dictionary_, 1982, p.476

Curriculum. There it stands in our college catalogs in its Latinate elegance, wrapped in the drab
cloak thrown over it by Scottish university faculties
in the last century. Who would recognize within these
colorless lists of courses, ranked in solemn order
within discrete departments, the daring, noisy, jos-
tling chariot races of the Roman circus?

The etymology of "curriculum" suggests at least
three meanings that are relevant to this discussion of
education, and connotes an excitement that is rarely
heard when curriculum is considered these days. The
curriculum was a way of behaving, the act of running,
indeed, "on the double." It was also the grounds where
the race took place, the field on which men could
display their talents. It meant, as well, the vehicle
employed to display those talents, specifically the
chariot used in the race.   What it did not mean, but
has come to mean, is the recorded experiences of those
men who have been over the same ground before, their
behavior while there, any worthwhile skills they developed as they did so, and their thoughts about their
experiences. What is lacking in college curricula is
the sense of urgent participation by students who are
currently running the course. There is too frequently
the sense of being spectators in the stands rather than

testing one's mettle in personal encounter. For too many students, earning a degree is too much like collecting baseball cards, so many from each team (department), in each league (division or school), with the data about each neatly inscribed (blue books and papers) on the back.

This is, of course, a caricature, but we recognize the truth within the exaggeration. I want to suggest that the way forward in curriculum development, and particularly in general education, is to recover more of the sense of activity, challenge, urgency, and personal involvement that the word curriculum originally conveyed. This has, in fact, happened in the Paracollege and is a consequence of the educational processes at the heart of the innovation. What those processes are have been described earlier in this book. What I wish to present here is something of the theory underlying the curriculum, and a few examples of seminars that have been based on the theory.

MORE THAN THE 440

A curriculum that aims to diversify students' ways of behaving must require more of them than a series of laps around the same track. The vehicle may differ, but if the same skills are required in every vehicle, (come to class, take the notes, read the texts, write the papers, pass the exams), the result will not be a broadly educated man or woman possessed of diverse skills and abilities, but men and women who have become very skilled through constant practice of a useful but narrow range of activities, such as taking notes, reading books, writing papers, and passing exams. Students admitted to selective institutions usually possess these skills to a high degree already. Can we do no better for them than to send them over the same track again, this time in a vehicle a bit more complex and more difficult to control? That refinement should occur in graduate study, the professional circuit.

Education that requires students to take courses of the same length, using essentially the same skills in each course, is like entering students into the same race time after time. I would prefer a curriculum to look more like a cross-country steeple chase over wide, broken ground. Running more efficiently in a circle will not win the prize here. Plotting one's own best route to the goal should be necessary. The terrain itself should require students to devise different ways of meeting different challenges along the way. They

70

should not make it to the finish line without trying some new techniques, making some unfamiliar moves, stretching and taxing themselves in ways not required in a short sprint over level ground. They should reflect on their own experiences as they go, altering their tactics as they assess their progress, their increasing skills, and their emerging ambitions. I have discussed the challenges students must meet. in the Paracollege in Chapter Two. To extend the metaphor, in this chapter we will consider the curriculum as chariot, the vehicle that carries the student even while she learns how to direct it toward her goal. If the image of a woman driving a chariot is disconcerting, it is still in a sense appropriate. It is the classical masculine "curriculum" that feminist critics are driving in a new direction. In this chapter I will suggest what a new feminist-driven vehicle of general education might look like, and offer three examples of inclusive seminars developed through the Paracollege.

CRITIQUE OF GENERAL EDUCATION

Three powerful forces have converged on the curriculum in the last thirty years that promise to recast its overall shape, and particularly the shape of general education. All three have focused criticism on positivist models of science and the epistemological assumptions that have dominated the disciplines for the past one-hundred years. Michael Polanyi (1958) and Thomas Kuhn (1962) have restored the person as knower as inalienably central to scientific investigation and conclusions. Sociologists of knowledge, such as Thomas Luckman and Peter Berger (1962), have persuasively argued the point that knowledge is a human product that reflects the time, place, and culture of those who produce it. Knowledge, they suggest, does not just fall like ripened apples off the tree of knowledge; it is produced by the careful husbandry of scholars who have pruned, mulched, sprayed and thinned in accord with the interests of their disciplines, current paradigms, and the market-place, including the market-place of ideas. Scholars such as Gerda Lerner (1979), Evelyn Fox Keller (1985), and Elizabeth Minnich (1981), among many others, have documented how those scholars tending the tree of knowledge have used assumptions and practices that have systematically kept women out of the garden. One of the consequences of women's exclusion is that what is marketed as general knowledge, acquired by the labor of men, inevitably reflects the interests of men and usually excludes the experience of women, whose interests have been presumed by men to be either the same as their own, or not worthy of consideration.

The implications of these criticisms are several. On one level they relativize the claims of those who assert that the fruit of their labors has a metaphysical status, an objectivity that places it beyond the fallibility of the time-bound, culture-embedded mind. Those scholars who have written and taught using a positivist model of knowledge must now own their conclusions as tentative, as models of reality, no less useful for that, but more susceptible to discussion, modification, improvement, and obsolescence than they previously conceded. Any who may have thought their methodologies granted them epistemological privileges that set them apart from the common table have been invited back to the general discussion. The realization that knowledge is perspectival authorizes a wider participation in its creation than was formerly the case. This does not require the conclusion that there is no truth to be known, or that all perspectives are equally valid interpretations of the truth. (That I have a perspective regarding the truth does not mean it is a perspective of nothing at all; but neither does the fact that it is my perspective exclude it from criticism as possibly based on very limited experience, personal taste, myopic vision, or faulty logic.) To the extent that knowledge which purports to describe the human condition is based on studies that have excluded the experience and perspectives of the one-half of the human race that is female, that knowledge is at least suspect as to its validity and generality.

These crititiques have radical implications for what is taught as general education and how it is taught (pedagogy) as well. If general education is about the common experience of men **and** women, then curricula that center on the experiences of men as remembered, recorded, and passed on by other men are inadequate to the task. If the curriculum of general education is flawed by its failure to be sufficiently inclusive of the experience of women (and of men and women of non-Western cultures and less privileged classes), then methods of teaching that emphasize the learning of <u>that</u> information as the end, telos, of education are also flawed. (Let us have no quibble here. For many students, passing an examination to satisfy a distribution requirement in general education is the end, the telos of the experience, whatever may be the more admirable long-range objectives of the teacher.)

Let us presume with Lionel Trilling that "the primary purpose of art and thought is to liberate the individual from the tyranny of his culture in the environmental sense and to permit him to stand beyond it in an autonomy of perception and judgement." (Trilling, 1965) If autonomy of perception and judgement is the ultimate goal of liberal education it is foolish to vitiate that autonomy through a Gradgrind system of pedagogy in which students "pass" by remembering and marshalling facts that the most pressing authority deems they must. (How does such a system further the autonomy of the student?) Teachers should be like guides rather than taxidermists. Guides teach skills necessary to the quest; if their guidance is based on their own active search for knowledge then students can eventually use the skills and tools to continue the quest on their own. The taxidermist, on the other hand, does not deal with a living, growing body of knowledge, but with a dead body, stuffing it to look natural, and offering the student the product of a quest instead of the process itself. The guide focuses on the interaction of student and environment; the taxidermist focuses on neither. Good guides make themselves obsolete because in time the students acquire their guides' skills and become, themselves, guides.

Students value teachers who guide by conversation, who are approachable, human, and personal in their pedagogy (Chickering, 1981, pp.648-649). Elizabeth Minnich contrasts conversation to rhetoric, the art of persuasion which dominates the contemporary academy. Rhetoric, she claims, "is the product of a speaker who stands before an audience. One is convincing: many are to be convinced." On the other hand,

> Conversation remains largely a private art: we do not have a tradition of teaching it. What happens in conversation? There is an exchange between people that actively involves both: A crossed monologue is not a conversation. Each speaker takes the other into account, asking questions, seeking words and ways to speak that can be heard by the other, listening with as much seriousness as speaking. What happens in conversation is between people. A good conversation is interesting--is inter, "inter-est" (Minnich, 1981).

Pedagogy that relies more on the dialogue of conversation and less on the monologue of lecture incarnates Ortega's concern that the student be the organizing principle of education, not the teacher and not knowledge abstracted from the activity and interest of the student (Ortega, 1946). It heeds Whitehead's criticism that we try to teach too many things rather than teach fewer things thoroughly (Whitehead, 1951). In conversation what is being understood and what is not quickly becomes evident; one it is clear when the reiteration of an idea belabors instruction to the point of pedantry and redundant effort. Conversation allows the exploration of an idea in combination with the ideas the student already possesses. It makes the student an active participant in intellectual exchange, a producer of insights, not merely a recipient of "inert ideas" (Whitehead, 1951). Such an approach to pedagogy is admirably suited to a situation in which the body of knowledge that traditionally has been taught is so flawed that it requires questioning and examination by those who teach it as well as by those to whom it is being taught.

INCLUSIVE GENERAL EDUCATION

In the Paracollege we have sought to develop a structure for general education that addresses what is truly general in human experience. In conversation with each other, in discussing books read, music heard, and art, film, and dance experienced together, the perspectives of both students and faculty are brought to bear on the experiences common to humankind. This structure for general education aims to help students develop their own capacities for perceiving, evaluating, and judging the material they study. It intends that students devise the habits of mind and heart to know themselves as the persons they are, immersed and embedded in their time and place, and embodiments of it, but at the same time to know that they participate in the construction of the knowledge by which they know themselves and their world.

This kind of general education should not be confused with general education courses that are designed to introduce the various disciplines of the academy. General education, as defined here, is not a prerequisite to, or introduction to, or preparation in any formal way for advanced work in the disciplines. General education in the Paracollege has its own assumptions and its own ends, ends that often are served by the disciplines but are in no sense defined by them.

General education contributes to human development within the larger frame of liberal education; it is not the whole body of liberal education, but it is its heart. General education occurs as students focus on experiences that are shared by most men and women. As those general experiences are brought into specific focus through the lives of men and women, ancient or modern, Western, Eastern, or African, their similarity to and difference from the students' and teacher's experience are noted. For example, dying and death are general human experiences. Aspects of these experiences differ from society to society, however, and change within societies. (Death and dying are public events in some cultures, for example, but are hidden from view in our society.) General education should highlight these elements of constancy, change, and difference. Study of such phenomena enables students to understand Henry Murry's dictum that all people are like all other people in some ways, like some other people in some ways, and like no other people in some ways (Murry and Kluckhohn, 1950). By refracting common human experience so that we see its permutations, general education enables us to see our experience as just that, our experience, and to assume an attitude toward it, and make judgements and act with regard to it.

What, then, are the common human experiences that a general education curriculum should investigate with its variety of disciplinary skills and pespectives? The list that follows is not exhaustive, but it has stimulated numerous topics for tutorials, seminars, and conversations in the Paracollege. As you read the list, consider what the disciplines you know best might contribute to such conversations.

COMMON HUMAN EXPERIENCES

1. Child birth
2. Nurture (early education/socialization)
3. Social institutions (tacit or unknown to their constituents)
4. Meaning quest (secular and religious responses to the mystery of being)
5. Biochemical interactions of human life and environment
6. Symbolic expression of experience
7. Dying and death

The list is by no means definitive; it needs additions and refinements. There are certain aspects of human experience in the late twentieth century that it seems to me might well be investigated in an inclusive program of general education. I would suggest such topics as the oppression of some human beings by others, the threat of nuclear annihilation, and the electronic mediation of experience. While these experiences are not general in the same sense as those in the list, their actual and potential impact on all of human experience is vast.

As you read over this list you may object that the categories are not mutually exclusive, not the province of any one of the disciplines alone. Nor, I suspect, is any aspect of general human experience. That is why general education ought not be conducted as a purely disciplinary endeavor. Life does not evolve according to the table of contents of a course catalogue. The knowledge and expertise and methods of several disciplines can fruitfully be joined in consideration of any of these topics. For example, childbirth is an experience with a history, a psychology, an anthropology, a physiology, a biology, a sociology, and, for some, a metaphysical aspect. Where there is childbirth there is woman; but there, necessarily, has also been man. How men and women at different times in different societies participate in the birth process is a fascinating study in which the best skills of many disciplines can usefully be brought to bear. It is a topic with relevance both in retrospect (since we were all born) but also in prospect, if we have hopes for the continuation of the species. It yields data from every continent, and reveals differences between classes and cultures within a continent. The biological changes that occur in our common transition from fluid-borne to air-breathing existence are fascinating, subtle, and rich in human drama.

Each of the seven topics listed has similar valency. Most of the disciplines of the liberal arts have contributions to make to the investigations of each. In the investigation, study, and conversation, the disciplines function as ways of framing questions and responses to a general human experience. The tutor-guide can demonstrate the power and limits of her discipline, and students can experience the importance of learning the craft, skills, and perspectives this guide has to offer. The student then has genuine reason for interest in learning the special skills of the disciplines and may elect to do so in further study.

We approach these common experiences with a set of questions designed to address the concerns from which a feminist critique of the curriculum arises. The questions inquire into the ways in which different individuals, while experiencing the same phenomenon, may experience it differently. Like the list of topics, the questions are meant to be evocative, not exhaustive.

QUESTIONS ABOUT COMMON HUMAN EXPERIENCE

1. What is similar about the way men and women experience this event?
2. How do these experiences differ for a man or a woman?
3. Are these experiences equally accessible to men and women?
4 . How are these experiences like and unlike my own when they are experienced by men and women of different classes, races, and cultures than my own?
5. How does the institutionalization of the experience affect men and women?

A list of common human experiences, confronted by questions such as these that inquire into issues of inclusiveness, continuity, similarity, and difference can provide criteria for organizing syllabi and selecting texts and other instructional resources in a wide variety of courses. (Later in the chapter we will look at two seminars that grew in this way.)

REFLEXIVE KNOWING

In analyzing and evaluating the varieties of general experience we obviously encourage a reflexive, perspectivistic method. We promote two kinds of reflexiveness, one personal and one structural. Personally, we want students to be self-conscious about the content, contexts, and process of their education. Students need to feel as well as understand the personal import of what they are studying. Structurally, we want students to see how disciplines create and package knowledge. If the central question of education is "What does it mean to be human in a particular time and place?" then a liberal education should examine the meaning of our meaning systems, specifically the disciplines and departments of academia. Part of the meaning of those disciplines derives from their historical development, and so we must study not just the discipline but the creation of the discipline. When did it originate? Who developed it? What were their aims and assumptions? Why were some people excluded in the making of the discipline? What have been consequences of that exclusion? By what canon or authority are they still excluded?

We also look for two kinds of perspectives in the new structure of general education. First, we encourage students to use the perspectives of the disciplines (including their characteristic questions and concepts) to analyze the general experiences of human beings. By doing so we are being self-conscious about the task assigned the disciplines "distribution requirement" model of general education. Second, we study the disciplines as disciplines (including the limitations caused by their exclusivity), and we focus primarily on questions about the disciplines rather than the concepts or conclusions derived by applying the disciplines. Those concepts are usually taught in other contexts, such as college courses and other Paracollege seminars and tutorials.

THE FRESHMAN SEMINAR

The one required course within the Paracollege is the Freshman Seminar. The seminar is two semesters long, is team-taught, and has been the setting in which we have had the most experience with the general education model discussed here. In the fall the seminar focuses on the common human experiences numbered three, four, and six in the list on page seventy-five. In discussion of the texts read, other general human experiences are also considered. The title of the seminar, "Naming the Mystery: Varieties of Human Experience Sometimes Called Religious," suggests broader objectives than a course in, for example, comparative religion. We consider how religions express, institutionalize, and at times challenge the values of a society. We observe how religious systems provide sanctions and options that differ for men and women in a society, and discuss the possible utility of such differences for the men and women concerned, and for the functioning of the society itself. We consider the assumptions a religion makes about human origins and destiny and note how these assumptions affect how people construct meaning in their lives. We want students to develop conscious, critical awareness of what they mean by "religious experience." Readings that examine both major and minor religious traditions are supplemented by films, videos, and art that reflect the experience of both men and women within those traditions.

The reasons why we introduce students into the Paracollege with a seminar on these themes are both philosophic and pragmatic. Students must have the equivalent of three courses in religious studies to graduate from St. Olaf. The Freshman Seminar introduces many of the themes and methods that they will encounter as they continue their study of religion at the college. On the philosophic side, students coming to college expect to be intellectually challenged. They will rise as high to a challenge as they are able, or sink as low as the standard the college sets for them. We try to set a standard in this introductory seminar that will challenge both the unexamined beliefs of conventionally religious believers and the attitudes of those who already have dismissed the study of religion as of no interest or importance in their lives. We expect the readings and discussions to evoke responses characteristic of the stages of dualism, multiplicity, and relativism that Perry identifies in the intellectual and ethical development of college students (Perry, 1970).

We have used texts such as Huston Smith's The Religions of Man, (the title itself provokes discussion!), the Book of Job, Achebe's Things Fall Apart, Silko's Ceremony, Fernea's Guests of the Sheik, Markandaya's Nectar in a Sieve, Weisel's Night, and Lagerquist's The Sibyl. We have read Dante's Divine Comedy, Dostoevesky's Brothers Karamozov, Milton's Paradise Lost, Shakespeare's King Lear. We have seen films such as "Yol" and videos such as "Playing for Time." Students read essays by Tillich, Bultmann, and Fromm to acquire knowledge of some approaches to the study of religious texts and phenomena. They write weekly papers that respond to the syllabus material as well the class discussions, and they exchange papers for mutual criticism. We regularly assign a book such as John Trimble's Writing with Style to be used in conjunction with all the writing students do in the seminars. We encourage students to write with good style and lucidity, and in our comments point out that the two are synonymous.

Discussions in the seminar have been spirited and are conducted at an unusually intense level. The introduction of questions regarding the cultural definition of men's and women's experiences and roles a society and our comparisons of these definitions in different societies have provoked the personal insights we hoped to encourage among the seminar students. They begin to see how their own sex, class, ethnicity, and religious traditions have shaped their perspective on what is real, of ultimate value, and meaningful to them. In the essays they write we see their own struggle to name the mystery in their lives.

The second semester of Freshman Seminar directly addresses the issue of what education in general is, and what general education in particular is. Students are told at the outset that the final project for the seminar will be a plan they each must devise for their own general education. They know that it must satisfy the Paracollege's requirement of "breadth" equivalent to courses taken for distribution in social sciences, humanities, fine arts, mathematics, and science. And they know that whatever plan for their education they devise they must provide a rationale for its appropriateness to themselves. With these goal posts set and boundaries demarcated, we enter into a semester of readings, lectures, and discussions designed to expand the students' awareness of the possibilities open to them.

As in the first semester, we have used a variety of texts and assignments to give focus and substance to the discussion. One of the readings that has worked well has been Friedenberg's The Vanishing Adolescent. Although the text is now nearly thirty years old, the experiences of the adolescents Friedenberg describes have by no means vanished. The text helps students understand themselves as people at a particular stage of development, and to see how high school experience was inimical to the legitimate needs and educational aspirations of the students in Friedenberg's study. Most contemporary students recognize their own experience in what Friedenberg describes. Those whose high school experiences were more satisfying find in Friedenberg's work a way to conceptualize what had made their experiences positive. Along the way, out of the corner of their eyes, as it were, students get a glimpse of one way in which social scientists investigate problems and draw conclusions.

Early in the second semester we ask students to write a short paper about their own most educational experience. We find--with no great surprise--that few students identify a classroom experience, but that all of them recount experiences that can be examined by disciplinary and interdisciplinary methods. This discussion of their own experience from the perspective of one or more disciplines clarifies the meaning of education, for better and for worse, in their own lives. Both this assignment and the Friedenberg book serve to revive in our students an impulse virtually suffocated by their high school education..to weigh ideas in the balance of their own experience. Regaining confidence in the value of their own experience is a necessary prerequisite to the evaluation of the uniqueness or generality of that experience. Before students can raise a question they have to discover that they have a voice.

We have used with real success Emerson's "The American Scholar" to extend the insights gained in the first assignments, and Lloyd Averill's "The Shape of the Liberal Arts" to expand the students' idea of what is both possible and desirable in general education. St. Olaf's centennial study, "Identity and Mission in a Changing Context" has served to allay any student's doubts about the college's support for the seemingly radical thoughts he or she is having, while Friedenberg's essay "Education" suggests the differences between schooling, education, and learning, and shows some ways of thinking about education that could maximize learning.

A major portion of the first third of the seminar is devoted to the discussion of the outstanding essays on education in Teaching As A Subversive Activity, by Neil Postman and Charles Weingartner (1969). Here under one cover students find support for many of the educational aims and policies of the Paracollege. Students are urged to acquire that "most subversive intellectual instrument--the anthropological perspective" that allows one to be an observer of one's culture even as one is a part of it. They are invited to understand the disciplines as "ways of knowing" the symbolic environment, the primary subject of study. They discover the rationale for the educational method employed in the seminar and throughout most of the Paracollege, which is that "the critical content of any learning experience is the method or process through which the learning occurs." Postman and Weingartner argue the importance of student-centered learning ("unless an inquiry is perceived as relevant by the learner, no significant learning will take place") and assert the importance of the inquiry method as central to the process of meaning making ("the art and science of asking questions is the source of all knowledge"). Because, they claim, language is both the vehicle of thought and the driver, education must be "language centered." Students need the languages of the disciplines (themselves social constructions) to unlock the meanings of particular social constructions of reality. (Postman and Weingartner, 1969).

Students at this point in the seminar have been challenged to consider the process of education they have experienced, with both its strengths and its weaknesses. They have measured their own experiences a-

81

gainst those of their classmates and against the possibilities and ends of education described in the assigned texts. They have been questioned about their own
aims in education, and have begun to form their own
ideas about what it is they seek in their education. At
this point the seminar leaders invite their colleagues
in the college to attend the seminar. They come to
answer students' questions about the kinds of questions
their disciplines ask, and to demonstrate or present
the kinds of answers their disciplines yield.

In sequential weeks students discuss the tools and
perspectives of sociology, psychology, history, art,
music, English, physics, and mathematics. These are
students who already have had a semester together asking questions about the roles of men and women in the
human quest for meaning. The experience of the seminar
has primed them to ask questions, and they usually are
full of questions as they begin to formulate their own
plans for general education. The discussions with the
disciplinary specialists are not monologues by faculty
barkers luring the gulls into their academic sideshows.
Rather, they reflect more of the spirit and intensity
suggested in the etymological roots of curriculum. The
students know why the curricular vehicles are there.
They want to know what it is like to drive them, and
where that sociological or mathematical chariot is apt
to take them. They want to know how long it has been
since this chariot had a thorough overhaul, and if the
faculty member has other models in the department. At
this point it is obvious that the students are not
sitting in the stands trying to hedge their bets, but
are already into the whirl of the action themselves.
Just when they stepped out of the stands and into the
arena is not clear; that they are behaving in ways that
show initiative, courage, and curiosity is indisputable. That they are making their education their own
cause is gratifying.

That is how the seminar works with the best of
them, and with most of them. Occasionally students
confess that they have grappled with the question "What
is general education?" and lost. Yet even these students submit proposals for their education that are
grounded in their own thinking, that consider the relationship of academic learning to their lives, and that
show an awareness of educational process that will
allow them to revise and improve their proposals as
they move through their college careers. Their feeling
that they have wrestled with the question and lost puts
them in league with most of the academic titans of

higher education. I suspect that Hutchins, Bell, Tussman, Eliot, Whitehead, Becker, Meiklejohn, and Ortega all knew that they learned from having struggled with the right questions rather than having stumbled upon someone else's right answer, and that their proposals were not the last word on the subject, but contributions to the continuing conversation.

BRANCHING OUT

The Paracollege has been a setting within which faculty from across the college have met to discuss and explore a wide range of educational issues. The Paracollege convened the faculty seminar that was the impetus for the development of the ideas about general education presented in this chapter. The discussion of feminist perspectives and general education begun there has borne fruit in other corners of the college's curriculum as well. It has given rise to team-taught courses jointly listed by two departments. Some bibliographies have been created, and in other cases have been revised, that are intentionally inclusive of women's experience and third-world perspectives.

One syllabus that deals explicitly with the roles of women in cross-cultural perspective was developed by Shoonie Hartwig, St. Olaf's Intercultural Liaison. The syllabus for her seminar incorporates the principle of asking questions about shared aspects of human experience. By asking these questions about life in other cultures the students gain perspective on their own experience and on the constraints and opportunities in their own lives. The heuristic nature of this design may be appreciated by examining the outline of the topics of the seminar.

A. Women as Believers

Belief systems shape our view of the world and who we are in it, our patterns of relationship, and our life expectations. Appropriate questions to raise within the context of any belief system are: Who or what is G-O-D? Who is in my world, and where do I fit? What is right or wrong, good or bad in this context? What can I expect from life? The cultures examined are Saudi Arabia, Israel, and the USA.

B. Women as Daughters, Mothers, Wives

The rhythms of life vary for men and women from culture to culture. What are those rhythms? What is expected of me in each of my roles? To whom and for what am I responsible? What is the time line of my life cycle? Chinese, Swedish, South American, and native American women are subjects here.

C. Women as Workers

In this section the effects of economics, politics, and education are considered as determinants of what I can and cannot do. Why do I need to work in this society? How do I acquire what I need? What are the obstacles to my acquiring it? Here life in the USSR, Cuba, Tanzania, and Germany are considered.

D. Women as Creators

Women have been, are, and can be agents of change, liberation, and transformation. Questions which must be asked in this context are: What is important? What are my dreams? What would I change? What are my choices? Who am I and what can I become? Who are my supporters? Such questions are raised about the life of women in Nigeria, India, South Africa, and the USA.

Such a seminar would contribute to the general education of any man or woman. It would be midwife to new perspectives on what it means to be a human being in our time. It would circumvent the education-as-trivial-pursuit method by requiring students to respond to enduring issues which have no simple answers. It would not depend on any one discipline but would provide models of how disciplines can be useful tools in life; it would show that the humanities and social sciences are not types of term papers but ways of knowing what we need to know.

Through the years the Paracollege has provided an on-going forum for the discussion of curriculum at the college. Sometimes the ideas generated there have been developed as Paracollege seminars. Sometimes they have appeared as courses in one or another of the departments of the college. Of even greater signficance, teachers who have shared in these discussions have had the opportunity, indeed, the obligation to examine with their colleagues the purposes of undergraduate education and the role that curriculum plays in it. In its development of curriculum the Paracollege has involved students and faculty in an educationally dynamic process that partakes of the rich associations of the very word "curriculum".

CHAPTER SIX

INSTITUTIONAL IMPACT

The quality of student faculty interaction,
both inside and outside the classoom, is the
more significant predictor of students' subsequent decisions to persist or withdraw from
college than the quality of the students' peer
relationships.
    Chickering, The Modern American College,
    (1981) pp. 649-650.

The establishment of an option such as the Paracollege can affect the operations of the whole college,
more so, of course, if the sponsoring college is relatively small. In this chapter we will consider how such
an innovation might affect the institution financially
through its influence on student recruitment and retention, and its possible consequences for curriculum and
faculty development in the whole institution. Finally,
we will examine some of the pitfalls into which the
Paracollege has stumbled and suggest some ways by which
other institutions might avoid these hazards.

FINANCES

The effect of the Paracollege on the budget of the
college was of great concern to the committee charged
with its evaluation in 1973-74. It was feared that a
program that relied so heavily on close interaction
between faculty and students might be exorbitantly
expensive. The review committee found, in fact, that
the operating expenses of the Paracollege made it only
about 3% more expensive than other instructional programs at the college. No new buildings had been constructed for administrative offices or for classrooms.
Additions to the library budget had not been necessary,
and, beyond those needed to serve the anticipated increase in the number of students, no new faculty had
been hired. Tutorials took place in tutors' offices.
Seminars were accommodated in existing classrooms. In
light of the positive consequences of the program the
slight additional cost incurred did not seem prohib-
itive.

The program was run then, and has been run since,
with a minimum administrative staff. The Senior Tutor
bears a one-half time administrative load; his other
half-time is as a tutor in the program and a teacher in

his department. A four-fifth's time Academic Co-ordinator handles the duties of a registrar for the program. A part-time secretary handles the typing and correspondence for the office and supervises the student help. The acquisition of computers in these offices has assisted the efficient discharge of their duties. The cost of operating the Paracollege has been kept low. Its operating budget is about that of a small department in the humanities at St. Olaf college. Contrary to what might be expected with regard to such an innovation, the Paracollege has never required the institution to invest large sums of money in its operation. It has satisfied those concerned with the financial "bottom line."

However, there have been financial benefits to the institution that could not have been computed during the first evaluation committee's study of the costs of the program. These benefits are the attraction and retention of students. The Paracollege has never had a student recruiting officer of its own; it has relied on the efforts of the college's admissions staff to let prospective students know that such an option exists at St. Olaf. While this contributes to the overall economy of the program, its wisdom has been questioned within the Paracollege when enrollments in the late seventies and early eighties reflected the decline in the general pool of traditional college-age students. Still, the policy has been to present the college as a whole to prospective students, and the Paracollege as one of the options within it that might make St. Olaf a more desirable choice for certain students. When the college's admissions staff is aware of the program, and when appropriate publications describing the program are made available to prospective students, the Paracollege has enrolled about all the students it is equipped to handle.

Each fall about fifteen students enroll at St. Olaf specifically because the Paracollege offers them an option they were unable to find in other colleges. In most cases these are students who did extremely well in high school and had been accepted at several colleges to which they had applied for entrance. In an era when competition for excellent students is keen the existence of an option like the Paracollege can have an important impact on recruiting, especially in an institution that depends heavily on student tuition to balance its budget. One might expect larger enrollments if a more focused approach to recruiting students explicitly for the program were undertaken, but such an advantage would need to be weighed against its increased cost, and against less tangible but no less important factors such as the disaffection of other elements within the institution which also might feel they merit special consideration in recruiting.

On the whole, this method of recruiting students for the innovation has been fair and effective; the Paracollege is not an institution unto itself. Its faculty's strength and diversity inhere in its being comprised of teachers from the various departments of the college. Furthermore, it is able to influence the educational effectiveness of the whole college through this intimate connection with the whole faculty. Students who select St. Olaf because of the Paracollege option are selecting the institution as a whole, but they are attracted by the particular way in which its resources are made available to them through the Paracollege.

At the same time a Paracollege-type innovation can enhance a college's ability to compete for excellent students, it can also help it avoid financial loss by retaining students who might otherwise transfer to another college. Students frequently have interests that legitimately can be met by a liberal arts faculty, but which can not be accessed in the limited number of courses offered. A student interested in 19th century American intellectual history and enrolled in a small college might find only one course in the philosophy department that appeared to pertain to his interests. In spite of the fact that there might well be faculty in the departments of religion, history, art, and literature whose education and interests equip them to offer tutorials on aspects of this field, if their skills and knowledge are not available to him that student may find it necessary to leave after only a year or two of study. Put another way, the instructional resources of most institutions are much richer than those described in their course catalogs. Students need not leave the institution, with the consequent loss of money expended to recruit those students, and of money to recruit replacements, if existing instructional resources were made more accessible through a paracollege-type innovation.

The cost of recruiting each student is relatively easy to compute; the more difficult but no less real costs are those associated with counselling and orienting students as they enter and leave the institution. How much more cost-effective it is, as well as humane, to retain students at a college they have chosen, to which they have adjusted, and within which they have made friends. My conservative estimate that twenty students each year transfer from the general college curriculum into the Paracollege rather than leave the institution translates to a financial savings of $200,000. each year in tuition and fees for every year those students remain at the college. Any particular institution would need to use its own tuition and fees, plus the costs for recruiting and orienting each student, and the cost of replacing each student who leaves before graduating when figuring its financial costs and benefits from an innovation like the Paracollege.

FACULTY DEVELOPMENT

I have already discussed the impact of the Paracollege on the personal and professional development of individual faculty members. What is the impact of the Paracollege upon the faculty of the institution as a whole? First, as with students, there are those faculty who are attracted to the college and remain because of the Paracollege. The Paracollege does not hire its own faculty, but draws its faculty from the departments of the college. Since it is important that teachers joining the college know that at some point they might be asked to represent their department in the Paracollege, as Senior Tutor I often interpreted the Paracollege to candidates for appointment. Not all prospective faculty were thrilled by the possibility of working at some time in the Paracollege. But many who were seriously committed to undergraduate teaching quickly recognized a rare opportunity for working closely with students. They saw both the chance to keep their own "brain children" alive through work outside their regular course assignments, and the advantages of working with colleagues in disciplines outside as well as within their department. For these, the Paracollege was an additional attraction to St. Olaf.

Some faculty admit that the Paracollege is one of their reasons for remaining at the college. "When I look at other teaching positions, I'm always discouraged that there's no Paracollege, and very few parallels to it," is how one colleague put it. Another states, "In the (Paracollege) curriculum areas and in its faculty as a whole there is a sense of shared enterprise that gives additional meaning to the classroom work." When I asked Paracollege faculty about how the Paracollege has changed them or their teaching the most frequent responses fell into two categories. One was a growing understanding and appreciation of faculty in other disciplines, an understanding that supplemented the satisfaction of teaching their subject with an increased sense of participation in the educational mission of the college. Second, Paracollege faculty frequently feel that their experience teaching in the Paracollege has enabled them to understand better how undergraduates think and feel. This understanding, they report, generalizes, making them more effective teachers in their college courses.

These are important sources of satisfaction for faculty working in the program, with important ramifications for their teaching throughout the college. Of far reaching importance for the college is the proportion of faculty throughout the institution who have gained such satisfaction and understanding. During the six year period I served as Senior Tutor some 70 faculty members worked in the Paracollege. Within the total current full-time faculty more than one-quarter of its members have had the opportunity to experience those challenges to their own development discussed in Chapter Four. These faculty have been involved in a faculty development program with profound potential to affect their contributions to the life of the college for many years to come. By their own accounts they have had to think more deeply and systematically about how their teaching relates to the work of their colleagues both in and outside their departments. They have in many cases made explicit what had previously been only an implicit understanding of their roles as educators. They acknowledge finding a renewed and sometimes a new understanding of how undergraduates learn. They have made friendships across the boundaries of their disciplines, friendships that have borne fruit in joint research and publications as well as in curriculum innovations. They have accomplished these things while "in the harness," not having been taken out of the life of the campus or sent to special courses designed for faculty development. Within but a few years more than one-third of the faculty in the college will have had this opportunity, a development that can only add pedagogical versatility and depth to an already strong faculty.

CURRICULUM

A subunit of the faculty organized as a Paracollege can provide a useful laboratory for initiating and refining innovations in the college's curriculum. It is possible for faculty to plan and teach seminars in the context of the Paracollege which they later can propose for inclusion in the course catalog of the college. In this sense the Paracollege serves a curriculum research and development function for the college. One innovation in inclusive general education and some of its ramifications for the larger college have been discussed in detail in Chapter Five. I will note here several other innovations together with suggestions for alternative ways in which a Paracollege might be adapted to the needs of a particular college or university.

The most easily identifiable affect of the Paracollege on the curriculum of the college is the adoption of courses developed within the Paracollege by the college's faculty. In these cases tutors in the Paracollege have offered tutorials and seminars on topics that were emerging as important areas in their disciplines but which had not been recognised as standard or important offerings in an undergraduate department. The tutors' work in the Paracollege enabled them to explore the emerging literature in the field, to conduct seminars that gave them experience with the topic, and to assess students' interest in such a course of study. Proposals that they eventually sent to the college's curriculum committee for consideration were, therefore, based on experience teaching the topic at the college. Courses in social sciences, natural sciences, art, and the humanities have been adopted by the college which have originated in the Paracollege. In some cases the faculty who developed these courses "took them with them" when their rotation in the Paracollege ended and they returned to their departments. In other cases faculty have developed a topic within the Paracollege and then have begun to teach it in the general curriculum while they remained in the Paracollege. In either case the Paracollege has provided a realistic setting for developing these new courses.

Faculty at the college who have not had a regular assignment to the Paracollege have noted the worth of such an opportunity to develop and try out new courses. Limited funds are made available to these faculty to prepare and teach one seminar in the Paracollege on a one time basis. In these instances the participating faculty member has substituted the seminar she was developing for one of her regular assignments in the department that semester.

Another way in which the Paracollege has enriched the St. Olaf curriculum has been its commitment to offer a limited number of seminars for a period of years to support students who are interested in Peace Studies and Environmental Studies. Both these areas of study include several departments and divisions in their scope. Many departments already offer courses that are relevant to these topics, but no one department is equal to the task of developing these areas of study without making serious inroads on its disciplinary course offerings. The Paracollege, by providing seminars and tutorials that require students to integrate their studies in these areas, allows general college students to pursue these topics along with their regular departmental majors. At the same time it allows Paracollege students to develop concentrations in these areas, drawing upon the courses offered in several disciplines and anchoring them in the integrative seminars, tutorials, and comprehensive examinations. There has been no need to initiate separate administrative structures to implement these opportunities for students; the Paracollege accommodates these studies within its general procedures for interdisciplinary studies.

The Paracollege has contributed to the college curriculum in a variety of other ways. One has been its training of faculty in the skills of interdisciplinary planning and teaching. The college inaugurated in 1980 a modified "Great Books" program for the general education of a limited number of freshmen and sophomores. Veteran Paracollege tutors were among those instrumental in planning the program. They have taught within it each year, and participated in its review and subsequent modifications. At least one department of the college has revised its introductory course offerings to take into account the ideas and pedagogical strategies devised by its representatives in the Paracollege. Many tutors report that they have modified the content of their general college courses to incorporate viewpoints and works to which they were exposed in the Paracollege. Four faculty have indicated that the focus of their sabbatical leave research has been directly influenced by work that they began while in the Paracollege. In each case this is research that will eventuate in changes in what they teach within the college.

OPTIONAL WAYS OF IMPLEMENTING THE INNOVATION

The Paracollege at St. Olaf College is designed as a four year option for undergraduate study that will satisfy all the requirements for a Bachelor of Arts Degree. This whole book is an argument in favor of such an option. In fact, however, the Paracollege also functions for some students as a two year general education program, for others as a means for developing an interdisciplinary major, and for others it functions as an honors program, enriching their departmental disciplinary major. A college interested in any of these options will find in the Paracollege a model worth investigating. Let us look first at the Paracollege as a vehicle for general education.

As I argued in Chapter Five, general education is not the same as an introduction to the disciplines. However, general education can be pursued by students in a program that uses the disciplines of the liberal arts to investigate enduring human problems. Within the Paracollege this investigation is based in a series of interdisciplinary, team-taught seminars in the humanities, social sciences, and natural sciences. These seminars are supported by offerings in tutorials, and the learning is integrated in the students' writing of examinations or papers that demonstrate their coherent, integrated grasp of the problems they have studied.

There are several advantages to students and faculty engaged in such a curriculum. Faculty are required to bring the skills of their disciplines to bear on a topic of general human concern. For example, colleagues and students alike hear and see how an historian approaches her work, the questions she asks, and how she weighs and evaluates her sources. Colleagues and students together see and hear how a philosopher, artist, or creative writer differ in their approaches to the same problem or period or question. The questions of what knowledge is, what its limits are, and what authority it confers are laid bare for all to consider. The skills of the disciplines are introduced; they can be developed later in courses designed for that purpose. Eight seminars in general education over the first two years of an undergraduate's career need not hinder the student already committed to a course of study. Rather, such an exposure to the interconnectedness of knowledge would probably be a most salutary corrective to a narrowly focused freshman or sophomore. While the full strength of the Paracollege innovation is in its four year framework, students can gain much from a general education that encourages interdisciplinary study in seminars and individual study in tutorials as well as course work within departments. Indeed, the habits of active participation acquired in the first two years might be expected to add strength to advanced study.

Colleges might consider the Paracollege's requirement of Senior Contracts, Comprehensive Examinations,
and a Senior Project as an appropriate model for an
honors program. Such an honors program could open the
area of interdisciplinary study to qualified students
from participating departments, or it might be a vehicle for advanced work by an undergraduate within a
department. In the former case a committee of teachers
drawn from each of the participating departments could
serve as a faculty of tutors, advisors, and examiners
for these students. A student could develop an area
concentration instead of a disciplinary major, or as an
addition to it. In the later case a Director could be
appointed from the department to work with these students, and members of the department could read the
comprehensive examinations and projects.

PITFALLS

The two most difficult problems in the operation of
the Paracollege have been variations of but one: time
management. When the problem affects students it must
be addressed through the sensitive but firm guidance of
the tutors who see the student week to week. When the
problem affects faculty it is related to the complex of
academic culture at the institution and the way the
particular faculty member accommodates institutional
values to her own personal and professional goals. It
is an over simplification in both instances to frame
the solution in terms of "work load management," that
inelegant phrase that conjures the image of sorting
bricks into wheelbarrows.

The deepest pitfall for students has been to mistake the flexible options for study within the Paracollege for lack of academic requirements. That there are
many paths up the mountain does not mean that there is
no mountain; neither does it mean that there are some
paths that require no effort to travel them. The Paracollege approach simply says that not everyone has to
take the same path, and that there are many valuable
experiences to be had along the way for the student who
is willing to get off the freeway. It is a kind of blue
highways approach to arriving at the required destina-
tion. I argue that the student will have a richer, more
subtly textured experience as he picks his own way
along. But the student does need to choose a path and
make progress.

There developed a kind of mystique in the early
years of the Paracollege about students who "floun-

dered" in their studies. Floundering was deemed probably a good thing, and perhaps even a necessary thing inasmuch as so many students seemed to be doing it. Case histories of some poor fish who managed eventually to flop up onto the beach and get on track to graduation were recounted as success stories. I am sceptical about the virtues of floundering. Most flounders, as I understand it, sink to the bottom of their murky environment and live out their lives largely unnoticed. They have given their name to metaphor because of the dramatic but ineffective behavior they exhibit when they find themselves "out of their depth." Students who are out of their depth, or in over their heads, need to be thrown a line and hauled out, or given close attention and support as they learn to tread water. What they don't need is more water. Faculty in programs like the Paracollege need to have some heuristic theory of instruction to help them assess the needs of students for support, challenge, stimulation, community, and mastery. Administrators of programs like the Paracollege must provide support for faculty who meet with students personally once a week, students who are adapting to the very real challenges of individual learning. Students who flounder in a class of fifty may continue quite unnoticed until midterm or the final exam. While faculty may truly care about these students they usually aren't confronted by them in their offices. Tutors are so confronted, weekly, and are often themselves in need of counsel on how to proceed with the student.

Faculty must also be given support in the management of their time in an innovation such as the Paracollege. That support must begin with the academic administration of the institution and must be honored through the leadership of divisions and departments. It is not enough for administrators to give lip service to the innovation. Whatever institutional rewards are given in the form of contract renewal, salary review, tenure, and promotion must acknowledge the contributions of faculty who work within the innovation. If this is not the case, faculty understandably will be reluctant to involve themselves in the innovation. Those who do so will be looking over their shoulders, apprehensive, trying to meet all of the institutional obligations that apply to them were they not working within the innovation. Faculty's time management, in such a situation, will mean their doing as little as possible in the innovation and counting the semesters until they have completed their rotation and can get back "on track" with their careers at the school. In

94

fairness to faculty, and ultimately to the students, it would be better not to venture such a program where the values expressed in the reward structures of the institution can not give it meaningful support.

At another level faculty time management requires that they be appointed to the innovation for a large enough percentage of their teaching time, and for a sufficient number of years, that they and the students with whom they work can become significantly involved. Our experience has been that appointments for less than one-third time (two course equivalents per year at St. Olaf) is an insufficient base for the program. The one-sixth time tutor can add needed breadth to tutorial offerings, or bring a special expertise to a seminar. These can be good experiences for the tutor, but are not adequate to sustain the development and supervision of seniors' comprehensive exams and projects, or the advising needed for the younger· students. A small core of faculty with one-half time appointments to the innovation is necessary to bear the burden of the general education program and to bear the brunt of senior advising. A larger group of one-third time faculty is needed to ensure that students have a range of subjects available for their study and tutors who have sufficient time to give them counsel regarding their study programs and to serve as readers of their examinations, papers, and projects. Arguments have been advanced in favor of a core of full time faculty for the Paracollege. The fate of such faculty in other cluster colleges often has not been a happy one. While it is true that full time faculty can give their undivided attention to the innovation, they can easily be perceived as redundant in times of financial duress. More important, their separation from the main body of the faculty vitiates the influence the innovation can have on the life of the institution. I doubt that the gains achieved by a full time core faculty outweigh the loss of involvement with the sponsoring college. If the institution is committed to the innovation, a half-time core faculty can provide the necessary direction and stability for the program. If the institution is not committed to the innovation, a full-time faculty component will not make it so.

Having addressed in broad terms the matter of faculty time needed for such a program, we can focus now on the issue of the individual faculty member's work load. As long as faculty comprehend their careers as teachers in terms of numbers of courses to be taught during a designated time period, (and this will surely be as long as the Carnegie Unit reigns in the realm of higher education) it will be necessary to devise some method to equate work in an innovative setting with work in the traditional one. The greatest complaint from faculty about work in the Paracollege is that there is so much of it. The equation we have devised to assess tutors' loads, five or six tutorials equals one course equivalent, makes a kind of rough sense in terms of "student contact hours." But it is very rough sense indeed. Tutorials in which the tutor is reading material for the first time along with a student are much more time consuming than tutorials on topics that are as familiar as one's own face in the mirror. In addition, there is a kind of intense, interpersonal attention that characterizes many tutorials that is quite different from that required in the lecture hall. Both kinds of teaching are difficult to do well, but the difficulties are not the same, and differ in degree for different teachers.

Furthermore, the challenges of working with students and colleagues in new ways, (which make the work difficult), are the very challenges that contribute the developmental impact of the program for faculty. Tutors must rethink and reformulate the ways they relate their knowledge and skills to others. That is an additional drain on an individual's energies, one that is not summarized in a calculation of the number of hours worked. I do not think there is a way around this difficulty. It might be eased if the institution appointed faculty to the program in sufficient numbers to reduce the rough equation to four tutorials equals one course, or set strict limits on the numbers of students who could enter the program. Still, the qualitative difference in the kinds of work required would remain.

The deepest pitfalls associated with the innovative program are those dug by committees. Tutors have complained about the number and length of committee meetings more than they have complained about any other aspect of the program. Because they are tutors in the Paracollege as well as members of departments and of the college, they face the possibility of triple committee assignments, a truly discouraging prospect for most faculty members. Over eighteen years, however, there has been an attenuation of the number and the duration of Paracollege meetings. In the late sixties and early seventies, when participatory democracy seemed the fate of every college committee, Paracollege meetings are reputed to have begun before dinner and lasted until midnight. Either the problems of the eighties are not so weighty, or the weighty ones were all solved, (or graduated). The Paracollege faculty now meets once a month for an hour and a half to conduct its business. Its committees meet when there are tasks to be done.

I am certain that a good deal of time is required in the early stages of an innovation's existence to sort out its procedures and policies. Once this is done, it would make greater sense to allot time for one person to administer these policies and procedures than to continue to weary the faculty with them.

I think the tutors' grievance about triple committee assignments, college, department, and Paracollege, is justified. Further amelioration of this problem probably lies in co-ordination between department Chairs and the Paracollege Senior Tutor in making committee assignments. This is another instance in which there must be agreement throughout the whole institution concerning the value of the innovation, lest a tutor's work in the innovation be treated as shirking departmental responsibilities. Tutors' work is not apt to be seen in this light if the innovation is interpreted to the whole college in terms of its broad positive impact on the life of the whole institution.

STUDIES OF THE PARACOLLEGE'S EFFECTIVENESS

Studies of the Paracollege's influence on student development began in the first year of the program's operation, the fall of 1969. The founding faculty committee thought it important that a data base be developed which could be used in evaluating the contribution the Paracollege made to the larger institution. Such data would enable decisions to be made regarding how to modify or even terminate the program after the initial funding phase had come to an end. One of the first assignments of the Office of Educational Research at St. Olaf was to acquire and analyze data about Paracollege students. These data were used by a committee of the faculty in 1973-74 to assess the effectiveness of the program in 1973-74. Minor modifications in the original plan for the Paracollege were based on this evaluation, and the Paracollege was given permanent status within the college by vote of the faculty in the Spring of 1974. Concern in the earliest studies was for the program's effect on students. While the influence of the Paracollege on faculty and institutional development was foreseen, these aspects have come under investigation only in the last few years.

STUDIES OF STUDENTS

The earliest studies of Paracollege students included assessments of their personality and intellectual development by the Omnibus Personality Inventory and the Cornell Test of Critical Thinking. Students' scores on the Scholastic Aptitude Test, their rank in their graduating high school class, and their grade point averages were included in the data. Their responses to questionnaires designed to assess their achievements in general education and changes in their religious, social, and political attitudes were also collected. Test scores of students on the Graduate Record Examinations were used to assess the comparative achievements of the Paracollege students with students' achievements in the general college program, using equal numbers of Paracollege and general college students matched in a pre-test and post-test design over three years.

The outcome, as reported by Troth and Farland (1974), indicated statistically significant gains over three years by Paracollege students in a variety of areas important for liberal arts students. One such area is the Intellectual Disposition Category (IDC) as measured by the Omnibus Personality Inventory (OPI). The IDC indicates a student's general level of interest and commitment to intellectual activity. The IDC is determined by examining the student's scores on four scales of the OPI, namely Thinking Introversion (TI), Theoretical Orientation (TO), Estheticism (Es), and Complexity (Co), plus the scores of scales measuring two supporting criteria, Autonomy (Au), and Religious Orientation (RO). The index derived from scores on these scales indicate a student's general readiness to be intellectually engaged, curious, and disposed to do the kinds of work associated with higher education. The authors of the OPI devised eight categories of Intellectual Dispostion, ranging from Category I, the highest, to Category 8, the lowest. The OPI, and the Intellectual Disposition Categories built from it, have been used extensively in research on students (see The Impact of College on Students, Feldman and Newcomb, 1969). It has been used to characterize the types of students attracted to different institutions, and to measure change in the intellectual disposition of students that might be attributed to their experience at college. In the St. Olaf studies, IDC scores were obtained for students entering the Paracollege and the general college as freshmen, and were obtained again from the same students at the end of three years of study in the two programs. Troth and Farland found that the Paracollege attracted students in the above-average Intellectual Disposition Categories (IDC 1,2,3,) to a signficantly greater degree than did the general college (p<.001). Further, at the end of three years the Paracollege maintained a higher percentage of students with above average IDC scores (p<.001). Indeed, eleven of the high scoring students from the general college freshman pool had transferred into the Paracollege program by the end of their Junior year, whereas only two of the original high scoring Paracollege freshman had transferred to the general program. Despite its being advertised as a program open to any student admitted to St. Olaf College, the Paracollege attracted and retained a signficantly greater percentage of intellectually oriented and committed students. In addition, students in the Paracollege program were more likely to make favorable shifts in IDC scores, or to maintain their high scores, than students in the regular program. This was particularly true for Paracollege women, who almost without exception displayed greater committment to intellectual pursuits after three years in the Paracollege.

An examination of the individual scales in the IDC Index reveals where Paracollege students made their most significant gains during their first three years in college. Paracollegians who were classified as "average" (IDC 4,5) as freshmen in their use of a logical, critical, scientific approach to problem solving increased their scores signficantly by their junior year (p<.01). Students who presented both average and high IDC scores at entrance on the scale that measures students' interest in and enjoyment of artistic pursuits (Es), increased their scores in this area signficantly (p<.05). This improvement was particularly significant (p.<.01) for women in the Paracollege whose scores between their first and third year greatly improved.

The last heavily weighted scale in the IDC is a measure of the student's openness to complex ways of thinking. High scorers reflect an experimental, flexible orientation in their approach to problems; they reject pat or standard answers to complex ideas or situations. Paracollege students who were average at entrance in their scores on the Complexity (Co) Scale, increased dramatically in this regard over three years (p<.01). Paracollege students initially high on this scale tended to maintain their above average rank (p<.05).

These statistically significant scores over three years by Paracollege students indicate that something associated with their participation in the Paracollege had an effect on their development not shared to the same degree by other students at St. Olaf or, indeed, by most students at other colleges included in Troth's and Farland's study. These two authors interpreted their data in a responsibly conservative way, attributing the differential changes over time between the Paracollege and other college groups to the accentuation of tendancies already within each group by virtue of the students' self-selection for one or the other of the programs. Stronger initial intellectual interests in the Paracollege freshmen group exerted peer pressures that were congruent with the faculty's educational aims for the program. Troth and Farland also argued that the experimental nature of the program would have attracted students with higher IDC scores. I would agree with their interpretation, but based on Astin's "mini-theory" of involvement and on further research on the influence of the Paracollege, I would argue that more than peer pressure is at work here. Important as peer culture is in the residential college, (and it is

very important), such a culture will not sustain itself, much less increase its force, if it is not supported, encouraged, and rewarded by the values of the
institution within which it is found. Douglas Heath's
research has dramatized the impact of faculty expectations, for good and ill, upon the initial academic
orientation of college students. (See "Implications of
Human Development for Undergraduate Teaching and Learning," Douglas Heath, Council of Independent Colleges
Summer Institute, June 1981).

In addition to the tests already mentioned, Troth
and Farland administered the Undergraduate Assessment
Program tests of achievement in humanities, social
sciences, and mathematics to twenty-four Paracollege
seniors. These seniors recorded mean scores that placed
them in the 96th percentile in humanities, 92nd percentile in social sciences, and 93rd percentile in mathematics and science.

On the basis of these findings the Paracollege's
case as a legitimate educational option was thought to
be sufficiently demonstrated. The faculty of the college voted to continue the Paracollege as a permanent
program of the college in the Spring of 1974, and the
program continued without further examination of its
effectiveness for several years.

In 1979 Dr. C. Robert Pace selected St. Olaf College as one of thirteen colleges to be used in the
pilot test of the final version of his College Student
Experiences Questionnaire. Included in the study were
three doctoral degree granting universities, two community colleges, three comprehensive universities, and
five liberal arts colleges. Included in the St. Olaf
College sample were 244 randomly selected students from
the general college and 152 of the 155 students then
enrolled in the Paracollege. (Three Paracollege students were off campus and unavailable to participate in
the study.) Pace's questionnaires were returned by 60%
(n=91) of the students in the Paracollege sample. The
two-tailed t-test was used to test the significance of
the differences of the means of the various subgroups
within the college and the differences between the St.
Olaf means and those of other colleges in the study. I
have not included data from the community colleges and
universities in the following data analysis; statisti-
cal comparisons are only with the other liberal arts
colleges in the sample. (I will report only scores of
Paracollege students; those interested in more information concerning the instrument or group data derived

from its use should contact Dr. Pace at U.C.L.A.).

The Pace study is of particular importance in the context of Astin's "mini-theory" of educational excellence cited in Chapter One. If involvement with one's studies is the critical factor in Astin's scheme, then measures of the extent of students' participation and effort expended in various academic activities should provide an index useful in assessing that involvement. Pace's instrument provides such an index. Pace's Student Experiences Questionnaire comprises fourteen scales of questions that probe for increasing levels of involvement or effort in fourteen aspects of college life. A few of the domains of college life which this instrument surveys are experiences with the library, faculty, courses, clubs and organizations, student acquaintances, and science laboratories. Students' responses to questions about their activities in these areas were assigned weights (very often=4, often=3, occasionally=2, and never=1). The degree of effort or involvement of a student in each domain was measured by totalling his score on a particular scale of questions. The mean scores for these activities were then analyzed acccording to demographic variables such as sex, year in college, relative grade point, and major.

These studies indicated that Paracollege students used the college library to a degree slightly above the mean of students in the other liberal arts colleges in the sample. Paracollege students who developed concentrations in the social sciences used the library to a significantly higher degree than those with other concentrations (p<.05).

As might be expected, Paracollege students reported significantly higher levels of involvement with the faculty than students in the general college or students at other colleges. This was particularly true of students in their second year or higher, and those earning grades of B+ or higher. Perhaps more surprising, given the Paracollege's emphasis on tutorial education, is that Paracollege students in the second year and beyond report a great involvement with the work of their regular college courses. An examination of items in this scale disclosed that Paracollege students were more likely to work at trying to see how different facts and ideas fit together, and to read additional materials about topics and ideas introduced in class than other students. This effort to integrate ideas and experiences, and to assume responsibility for furthering their own education, is one of the primary

103

aims of education in the Paracollege, and supports Troth and Farland's earlier finding that Paracollege students favored complex, analytical, critical thinking.

One of the reservations sometimes expressed about undergraduates assuming responsibiity for planning their own educational programs is that students will study only those things that greatly interest them rather than acquiring a broad liberal arts education. It is feared they will become prematurely specialized. It should be noted, however, that Paracollege students do not determine the breadth of their education; the Paracollege has breadth requirements in humanities, social sciences, science, mathematics, foreign language, religion, and the arts. What is true is that Paracollege students have more options regarding how they study material in these areas. In fact, Pace's study indicates that Paracollege students' involvement in the arts, music, and theater is significantly greater than that of students in any of the other colleges in the sample ($p < .05$).

Three scales in Pace's instrument measure students' involvement in activities at the student union, athletic facilities, and campus clubs and organizations. Involvement in such activities might be interpreted to indicate something of the breadth of general interest and social involvement of students on any campus. One would predict that students with narrow interests, campus "egg heads" and "grinds," would fall near the bottom of these scales. It is interesting to note, therefore, that Paracollege students, like their peers in the general college at St. Olaf, tend to make greater use of the student union than do students in the other colleges in the sample. Paracollege students tend to use the union as a place to hear speakers, and to attend meetings; rarely do they use it to play the games (pool, bowling, video games) available there.

Paracollege students were less likely to use athletic and recreational facilities than other students in the sample. Conversely, the only item in this scale where Paracollege students exceeded the score of other students was their likelihood to set goals for themselves in athletic and physical activity and to keep a chart or record of their progress in that activity. I attribute this, at least in part, to the fact that Paracollege students may satisfy their physical education requirement by proposing a program of physical activity for themselves that they must record and have certified. The rationale for such a requirement is that disciplines of physical exercise are important to general health and well-being; if such habits can be established in college they may carry over into the post-collegiate years when there are no physical education classes that require attendance. Pace's study suggests that Paracollege students do undertake this discipline; indeed, students with math and science concentrations did so at a significantly greater level than other Paracollegians (p<.05). Whether this discipline persists beyond the colleges years we do not know.

Paracollege students were slightly more apt to participate in clubs and campus organizations than were their general college peers, although St.Olaf students as a group tended to score slighly below the mean for all students in the study on this scale. This finding suggests that social clubs and activities play a generally less important role in the academic culture of St. Olaf College than they do at other schools in the sample. This may well be regarded as a good thing by the faculty, but be perceived as something of a problem by students who hope to find in college a setting for social activity rather than for academic work. On balance, it does not appear that Paracollege students restrict themselves to a narrow sphere either socially or intellectually, at least not to a degree greater than their general college peers.

The writing that students do in college is usually regarded as an important aspect of their intellectual and scholarly development. Clearly written, concise prose is regarded as a sign of well-organized thinking. The mean score for Paracollege students on Pace's scale that measures involvement in writing was significantly higher than for all other students in the sample (p<.05). Within the Paracollege sample, math and science majors, and those with grades of B plus or higher, indicated significantly higher involvement in writing (p<.05). I attribute these differences to the students' need to prepare written papers for their tutorials in every field; students do not cease to write when they complete a required Freshman English course. The use of those papers as the basis for discussion within the tutorial sessions means that what students write matters; it is not just an assignment to be completed. It will be discussed, refined, perhaps defended in the tutorial session. The content and the form of writing, in science as well as other fields is subject to scrutiny week after week. In addition, the requirement to write comprehensive examinations, portions of which may take the form of extensive integrative papers or research projects, provides an incentive for students to work toward the development of a high standard in their writing.

The subjects in the curriculum that have presented greatest difficulty for tutors over the years have been the sciences. Science tutors are accustomed to teaching sequential courses built upon previously learned materials. They are not accustomed to devising laboratory experiences for only one or two students. As a consequence many Paracollege students have elected to study science in the regular courses of the college, at least at the introductory levels. This, I think, accounts for Pace's finding that there was no significant difference in laboratory experiences for students in the general college or the Paracollege, with one exception. Paracollege students who developed concentrations in math and science had significantly greater experiences with laboratory learning than students with other concentrations ($p<.01$). My observation of these students suggests that they frequently had worked closely with their tutors on the tutor's research projects, and that in their senior year they undertook research projects of their own to fulfill the Senior Project requirement.

Faculty hold the hope that what they present in lectures or assign to be read is of sufficient interest to students that it engages their thought and conversation outside the classroom. In his study of Paracollege students Pace surveyed their topics of conversation outside the class or laboratory. What he found was that Paracollege students were slightly above the mean of other students in the sample in their discussion of intellectual, cultural, and science-related topics outside the classroom, and below the mean in their discussion of jobs, careers. money, popular music and social events. Paracollege students beyond the freshman year exemplified this finding at a significantly higher level than Paracollege freshmen ($p<.01$). This suggests that the Paracollege's modes of instruction succeed in engaging the interest and shaping the spontaneous thought processes of students. First year students in the Paracollege show no significant difference in this regard from other students; by the time they are upperclassmen, however, the difference is apparent.

Paracollege students assessed the quality of their relationships with their faculty more positively than did students at any other college in the sample ($p<05$). Here is evidence of involvement of a high order. Faculty may boast that their office has "an open door." It is quite another matter if students choose to go through it, and still another what they talk about when they do. Paracollege students report greater frequency of conversations with faculty, which might be expected from the modes of instruction used in the program. But students also report those conversations taking place outside as well as inside the classroom and faculty office, and topics of conversation moving beyond the official topic of the class to include concern for careers, personal interests, and problems. As was noted in the chapter on student development, such interaction is associated with excellence and a high degree of influence in teaching.

The Pace instrument asked students to assess their own development in different areas of study. More than two-thirds of the Paracollege students reported they had developed "very much" or "quite a bit" in the areas of general education, art appreciation, literature appreciation, clear writing, philosophy/culture, personal thinking, synthesizing information, and finding information. Another indication of the effectiveness of the educational processes in the Paracollege is that significant differences between the reports of freshmen and of upperclass students in the Paracollege were found in the areas of general education, philosophy/culture, personal values, self-understanding, critical thinking, synthesizing information and finding information. The educational processes that characterize the Paracollege effect desired changes in its students over their years in the program.

The research by Troth and Farland confirms the power of the Paracollege to affect change in its students as measured by standardized tests. The data from Pace's study point to a high degree of involvement of Paracollege students with their studies, the "cornerstone" of Astin's "mini-theory" of educational excellence.

STUDENT SATISFACTION

In the fall of 1981 I undertook a study of the attitudes and experiences of students then enrolled in the Paracollege. The Office of Educational Research at St. Olaf helped prepare a survey instrument which was sent to all students then currently standing for their degree in the Paracollege. There was a response rate of 69% (N-79). My hope was that the survey would identify areas of weakness in the program that we could devote

107

our efforts to strengthening. The strategy was to identify students who expressed general dissatisfaction
with the program, and then to analyze the specific
factors in these students' experience that would account for their dissatisfaction.

To the global question, "All things considered,
how satisfied are you with the Paracollege?" 39% responded, "Completely satisfied," 58.4% responded "Somewhat satisfied," and only one student each reported
being "somewhat" and "completely dissatisfied." I was,
frankly, amazed at the degree of satisfaction the students reported. Of course inasmuch as no one requires
students to enroll in the Paracollege this high degree
of satisfaction may simply reflect the process of self-
selection in the program. Students who are dissatisfied
may transfer to the general college program with relative ease. Still, this was a strong endorsement by the
students; an examination of the specific items within
the survey indicated why. Ninety-eight percent reported
that their academic work was meaningful to them; only
one percent "disagreed somewhat" that this was the case
for them. Such a finding reverses the meaning of the
epithet "merely academic!" School work, rather than
being a chore to be gotten through before getting down
to the serious business of dorm life and weekends, was
a source of meaning and satisfaction for these students.

Another reason they so strongly endorsed the Paracollege program was their discovery that they were
known and respected as persons. Ninety-six percent of
the respondents agreed that in the Paracollege there
was concern for them as individuals. Eighty percent
affirmed that their Paracollege tutors were more helpful than other advisors they had had. Eighty-three
percent "strongly agreed" that their involvement in the
Paracollege was worth the time and effort they had to
put into it; another sixteen percent "agreed somewhat."
These are impressive evaluations by students still in
the midst of a program that demands much of them by way
of individual initiative and diligent independent study. Indeed, I would argue that it is this very opportunity to design and follow a course of study that interests them, and the consequent necessity to work hard
and creatively to integrate those studies that is the
primary reason for the students' high degree of satisfaction in the program.

It might be asserted, on the other hand, that high
levels of satisfaction reflect a kind of Hawthorne

effect; the students surveyed rising to the occasion and presenting their very best (and very biased) self-report on these items. If this were the case, however, one would expect surveys of campus life generally to reflect a similar rosy glow wherever they are conducted. This was not the case where identical survey questions were asked on other campuses. (See reports of the American College Testing Service.) While this student generation is not chanting "Do not fold, mutilate, or spindle" in registrars' offices across the land, they generally do not lack a catalog of grumbles and complaints. In contrast, our attempt to elicit such a catalog from Paracollege students produced instead a litany of appreciation.

PARACOLLEGE GRADUATES

As part of an evaluation of the Paracollege carried out in 1981-82 I surveyed all the alumni who had ever graduated from the Paracollege. With the assistance of the Office of Educational Research an instrument was devised which included a series of questions regularly asked of alumni on nationally normed survey instruments. My aim was to find out what Paracollege students were doing after graduating, and how they assessed their education now that they had experience in the larger world. The response rate was 70 percent (N=229).

What struck me as I reviewed the results of this survey was the diverse number of things that Paracollege alumni were doing. Paracollege graduates occupied seats as diverse as a judiciary bench and a dairy milking stool; their jobs ranged from editor of Vogue magazine to a community advocate in a church-supported poverty program. The individual interests developed in their undergraduate years seemed to have been extended into their post-graduate occupations. This rich diversity of employment is only hinted at in occupational categories. Still, it is of interest to note the general proportions of graduates working in different fields.

TABLE 1

What is your area of employment?

Professional, technical	44%
Administrative, managerial	13%
Farming, forestry	1%
Sales, Clerical	8%
Service	10%
Other	23%

One alumnus, now practicing law, reported that the skills he acquired in the Paracollege--defining a problem, deciding how best to research the problem, integrating the viewpoints of several different disciplines in understanding the problem, working independently, but ultimately being able to communicate his ideas to other people, had all been exercised and developed during his years in the Paracollege.

Indeed, the skills these alumni acquired when, as Paracollege students, they defined a concentration, and prepared comprehensive examinations and a senior project are similar to those required of students in most graduate programs. It is not surprising, then, that many Paracollege graduates have earned advanced degrees. In 1981 forty percent of the 229 alumni who responded to the survey had earned advanced degrees since the first class had graduated in 1973. Fifty-one had earned Masters Degrees, seven Doctors of Philosophy, twenty-five had earned professional degrees, and nine had earned other advanced degrees. The alumni's assessment of their preparation in the Paracollege for advanced work is shown in Table II.

TABLE II

How well did St. Olaf prepare you for your continuing education?

very well	57%
more than adequately	23%
adequately	20%
less than adequately	1%
very poorly	0%

Here is an answer to those who are concerned that undergraduate preparation in other than the traditional disciplines is a risky proposition for those who aspire to advanced study. I see these figures as confirming Douglas Heath's assertion that colleges fail to substantially influence students because they fail sufficiently to challenge them, especially to challenge them in the first weeks of their academic careers (Heath, 1981). Students are capable of accomplishing much more than is usually expected of them. Indeed, they come away from high school to college seeking and needing challenges that will require them to think, feel, and behave in more mature ways, ways which we presume in graduate students but are reluctant to cultivate in undergraduates.

We asked alumni to specify the ways in which their Paracollege experience had benefitted them. As Table III shows, alumni found their greatest gains in those areas in which the Paracollege had required the most from them. The questions concerning personal gains were not, in most cases, about specific subject areas; we wanted to assess the alumni's overall sense of how their college experience had prepared them for life in the larger society.

TABLE III *

How much did your education in the Paracollege contribute to your personal growth in each of the following areas?

	Very much	Somewhat	Very Little
Writing effectively	52%	39%	9%
Working independently	87%	12%	1%
Understanding written information	50%	43%	7%
Learning on your own	88%	11%	2%
Planning and carrying out projects	69%	29%	3%
Persisting at difficult tasks	59%	34%	7%
Defining and solving problems	52%	43%	4%

*(Rounded to nearest whole percentage; totals may exceed 100%)

The strongest reported gains were in working independently, learning on one's own, planning and carrying out projects, defining and solving problems, and learning to persist at difficult tasks. These are widely transferable skills, important in practically any setting in our society, whether academic, professional, or

111

domestic. A person with these skills is the autonomous, independent, critically thoughtful, problem-solving individual who is highly prized in the hierarchy of American values. Development of these skills without commensurate gains in human sensitivity and compassion could just as well produce an emotionally cold, driven, technocrat. It was with deep pleasure, therefore, that I noted a second level of gains by these alumni reported in Table IV.

TABLE IV *

How much did your education in the Paracollege contribute to your personal growth in the following areas?

	Very much	Some what	Very little
Understanding different philosophies and cultures	49%	45%	6%
Understanding the interaction of man and the environment	35%	43%	22%
Recognizing assumptions, and making logical inferences and reaching correct conclusions	39%	55%	6%
Understanding and appreciating the arts	53%	38%	9%
Broadened aesthetic sensitivity	58%	34%	8%

*(Rounded to nearest whole percentage; totals may exceed 100%)

Here we note that alumni report increase and broadening of their aesthetic sensitivity, understanding, and appreciation of the arts; increased understanding of the interaction of man and the environment; broader understanding of different philosophies and cultures; and an increased ability to recognize assumptions and make logical inferences and correct conclusions. In these gains we see the importance of those subjects traditionally incorporated in the liberal arts. These reports are important evidence that programs such as the Paracollege that combine required areas of study with varieties of ways in which they may be studied do achieve the aims of liberal arts education without slavish adherence to the standard course format and sequence.

Some of the areas in which alumni reported the least gains are areas in which the Paracollege had made no attempt to teach; others indicate less effectiveness in certain subject areas than we had hoped or with which we could be satisfied. Alumni's reports of gains were not all we hoped they would be in the areas of learning to speak effectively, understanding graphic information, working co-operatively in groups, understanding and applying mathematics in one's daily life, leading or guiding others, and understanding and applying scientific principles and methods. In all except one of these areas the majority of alumni did report having gained "very much" or gained "somewhat."

TABLE V *

How much did your education in the Paracollege contribute to your personal growth in each of the following areas?

	Very Much	Somewhat	Very little
Speaking effectively	22%	53%	25%
Understanding graphic information	8%	55%	38%
Working cooperatively in a group	20%	52%	28%
Understanding and applying mathematics in your daily activities	7%	28%	66%
Leading/guiding others	15%	51%	34%
Understanding and applying scientific principles and methods	21%	53%	26%

*(Rounded to nearest whole percentage; totals may exceed 100%)

The areas of scientific learning and interpersonal communication and leadership are crucial components in a modern liberal arts education, and we have taken steps to correct these weaknesses. We have revised the general education offerings in mathematics and science, and have added a tutor from the area of speech and communications to the Paracollege faculty. (There had been no tutor in this area from the beginning of the program.) As noted in Chapter Five, the area of scientific education has been perhaps the most challenging aspect of the curriculum to adapt to Paracollege modes of instruction.

We were interested to assess how effectively the

habits of mind and behavior cultivated during the college years carry over into the lives of graduates once they leave the campus. Accordingly, we asked a series of questions regarding how alumni spend their leisure time. We were pleased to discover that ninety-one percent of the alumni reported that they were currently working on a study/learning project. Eighty-three percent indicated that they had completed within the past year a piece of work (written, graphic, musical, artistic, theatrical) that they found satisfying or creative. Further, sixty-seven percent reported that they contribute volunteer work to community groups and activities (political, civic, religious, artistic, educational). What these reports signify to us is that the interests students develop during their college years are not hung in the back of the closet with the cap and gown, but continue to animate the thought and work of graduates after they leave the college. That the qualities and values of the liberal arts continue to be important aspects of these persons' lives, is, perhaps, the most telling evaluation of the program that can be made.

When asked to respond to the question, "Regardless of the financial benefits, has your college education improved your quality of life?" more than eighty-eight percent responded "definitely yes;" nearly ten percent replied "probably yes." Less than two percent reported being "uncertain" if this were the case. No alumni reported that their lives had not been qualitatively improved by their having pursued the education they had.

It is this general level of positive regard for their experience in the program that accounts for the alumni's response to the question, "If you could start college over, would you choose to enroll in the Paracollege?" Fifty-nine percent reported "definitely yes", and another twenty-four percent replied "probably yes." Eleven percent were uncertain, while four percent said "probably no." Only one percent (N-3) said they "definitely" would not repeat their Paracollege experience.

Here, again, is evidence that undergraduate education can be a meaningful and satisfying experience while it is being undertaken, and that its rewards in terms of quality of life are worth the time and energy invested. Genuine gains in academic competence as measured on nationally normed tests can be achieved by students in programs such as the Paracollege. The work necessary to accomplish those gains is perceived as meaningful and worthwhile by the students while they are in the program, and continue to be highly valued by graduates of the program. What more could an alumni office or college development officer ask? Faculty who work within the program report that their teaching has improved and become more satisfying, that their understanding and appreciation of students has been broadened, that they have a new appreciation for the way their own discipline relates to the aims of the liberal arts, and that they know and have friends outside their own disciplines within the college as a consequence of participation in the program.

In Chapter One I cited John Gardner and Alexander Astin who challenge higher education to strive to enable self-discovery and personal development within each student. In their view it is an institution's ability to evoke and support such change that distinguishes it as excellent. It has been my thesis that when a college accepts this challenge it will make of itself a community in which teachers as well as students will pursue "self-discovery (and) perpetual reshaping" in quest of "the best self, the best person" they can be (Gardner, 1961, p.136).

In the Paracollege we may see a model of excellence, an academic community that has demonstrated its worth and its power to affect positive change in the lives of students and faculty. While other innovations have succumbed to economic and demographic changes during the past two decades, the Paracollege has demonstrated its viability in American higher education. It deserves to be studied, and certainly can be emulated with benefit to students, faculty, curriculum, and institution alike.

REFERENCES

Achebe, Chinua, Things Fall Apart. New York: Bal-
lentine Books, 1983.

Anderson, Margaret L. Thinking About Women: Sociological and Feminist Perspectives. New York:
Macmillan, 1983.

Astin, A.W. Four Critical Years: Effects of Col-
lege on Beliefs, Attitudes, and Knowledge. San
Francisco: Jossey-Bass, 1977.
_____, "Involvement The Cornerstone of
Excellence." Change Magazine, July/August 1985,
pp. 35-39.
_____, Education for Excellence. San Francis-
co: Jossey-Bass, 1985.

Averill, Lloyd, "The Shape of the Liberal Arts."
Audio cassette available from National Public
Radio.

Becker, Ernest, Beyond Alienation. New York: Bra-
zilier, 1967.

Berger, Peter, and Luckman, Thomas, The Social
Construction of Reality. New York: Doubleday,
1966.

Berry, Elvera B. "Student-Faculty Interaction:
Design or Default." Paper presented at the
National Conference on Higher Education, spon-
sored by the American Association for Higher
Education, Tuesday, March 19, 1985.

Boorstin, Daniel, An American Primer. NAL, 1968.

Bloom, Alan, The Closing of the American Mind. New
York: Simon and Schuster, 1987.

Chickering, A.W. Education and Identity. San Francisco: Jossey- Bass, 1969.

_____, and Associates, The Modern Ameri-
can College: Responding to the New Realities of
Diverse Students and a Changing Society. San
Francisco: Jossey-Bass, 1981.

Douglas, William O. Go East, Young Man, The Early
Years The Autobiography of William O. Douglas.
New York: Random House, 1974.

Emerson, Ralph W. "The American Scholar," in Boorstin, Daniel, An American Primer. NAL 1968.

Erikson, Eric H. Childhood and Society. New York:
Norton, 1964.

Feldman, K.A. (Ed.). College and Student. New
York: Pergamon, 1972.

Feldman, K.A., and Newcomb, T.M. The Impact of
College on Students. San Francisco: Jossey-Bass,
1969.

Fernea, Elizabeth, Guests of the Sheik: An Ethno-
logy of an Iraqui Village. New York: Doubleday,
1969.

Freedman, Mervin, et al. Academic Culture and
Faculty Development. Berekeley: Montainge Press,
Inc, 1979.

Friedenberg, Edgar Z. The Vanishing Adolescent.
New York: Dell, 1959.
_____, "Education," in American Quarterly,
Spring/Summer, 1983.

Gaff, J.G. Toward Faculty Renewal: Advances in
Faculty, Instructional and Organizational Development. San Francisco: Jossey-Bass, 1975.

Gaff, J.G. (Ed.). New Directions for Higher Educa-
ion: Institutional Renewal Through the
Improvement of Teaching, no. 24, San Francisco:
Jossey-Bass, 1978.

_____, and Gaff, Sally Shake, "Student Faculty
Relationships." In Chickering, The Modern
American College. San Francisco, Jossey-Bass,
1981.

Gardner, John W. Excellence: Can We be Equal and
Excellent Too? New York: Harper and Row Publish-
ers, 1961.

Gonnerman, Fredrick H. "Paracollege at St. Olaf
Today", Saint Olaf, Vol. 34, No., 3, June, 1986,
pp. 6,7.

Gould, R. Transformations: Growth and Change in Adult Life. New York: Simon and Shuster, 1978.

Heath, D.H. Growing Up In College: Maturity and Liberal Education. San Francisco: Jossey-Bass, 1968.
_____, "Implications of Human Development for Undergraduate Teaching and Learning." Address given at Council for the Advancement of Small Colleges Summer Institute, Peoria, Ill., June 1982.

Hong, Howard, et al. Integration in Christian Higher Education. St. Olaf College, Northfield, Mn., 1956.

"Identity and Mission in a Changing Context." St. Olaf Information Services, St. Olaf College, Northfield, Mn. 1974.

Jaggar, Allison M. and Struhl, Paula Rothenberg, Feminist Frameworks. New York: McGraw Hill, 1978.

Jones, Richard M. Fantasy and Feeling in Education, New York: New York University Press, 1968.

Kegan, Robert, The Evolving Self: Problem and Process in Human Development. Cambridge, Ma.: Harvard University Press, 1982.

Keller, Evelyn Fox, Reflections on Gender in Science. New Haven: Yale University Press, 1985.

Kuhn, Thomas, The Structure of Scientific Revolutions. Chicago: University of Chicago Press, 1962.

Lagerqvist, Par, The Sibyl. New York: Random, 1958.

Lerner, Gerda, The Majority Finds Its Past: Placing Women in History. New York: Oxford University ty Press, 1979.

Levinson, D. J. and others, Seasons of a Man's Life. New York: Knoph, 1978.

Markandaya, Kamala, Nectar in a Sieve. New York: The New American Library Inc., 1954.

119

Martin, W.B. <u>A College of Character: Renewing the Purpose and Content of College Education</u>. San Francisco: Jossey-Bass, 1982.

Minnich, Elizabeth, "A Feminist Critique of the Liberal Arts." In <u>Liberal Education and the New Scholarship on Women: Issues and Constraints in Institutional Change, A Report of the Wingspread Conference</u>, 1981.

Murry, Henry, and Kluckhon, "Personality Formation: The Determinants." In <u>Personality in Nature, Society, and Culture</u>. New York: Alfred A. Knopf, 1950.

Neugarten, Bernice, "Adult Personality: Toward a Psychology of the Life Cycle." In <u>Middle Age and Aging</u>. Chicago: University of Chicago Press, 1968.

O'Reilly, Mary Rose, "The Peaceable Classroom," <u>College English</u>, January, 1984.

Ortega y Gasset, <u>The Mission of the University</u>. London: Kegan Paul, Trench, Trubner, 1946.

<u>Oxford Dictionary of English Etymology</u>. Oxford: The Clarendon Press, 1985.

<u>Oxford Latin Dictionary</u>. Oxford: The Clarendon Press, 1982.

Pace, C.R. <u>Measuring Outcomes of College: Fifty Years of Findings and Recommendations for Future Assessment</u>. San Francisco: Jossey-Bass, 1979.
_____, <u>College Student Experiences</u>. San Francisco: Jossey-Bass, 1979.

Parker, C.A. (Ed.) <u>Encouraging Development in College Students</u>. Minneapolis: University of Minnesota, 1978.

Perry, W.G. <u>Forms of Intellectual and Ethical Development in the College Years</u>. New York: Holt, 1970.

Polanyi, Michael, <u>Personal Knowledge</u>. Chicago: University of Chicago Press, 1958.

Postman, Neil, and Weingartner, Charles, <u>Teaching as a Subversive Activity</u>. New York: Dell/Delta,

1969.

Rice, R. Eugene, "The Academic Profession in Transition: Toward a New Social Fiction." Teaching Sociology, 1986, Vol 14, January pp. 12-23.

Rudolph, F. The American College and University. New York: Vintage Books, 1962.

Sanford, R.N. The American College. New York: Wiley and Sons, 1962.
_____, Where Colleges Fail: A Study of the Student as a Person. San Francisco: Jossey-Bass, 1967.
_____, Learning After College. Orinda, Ca.: Montaignne, Inc., 1980.

Seely, John, "University as Slaughterhouse." In Great Ideas Today. Chicago: Encyclopaedia Britannica, 1969.

Sheehy, G. Passages: Predicatable Crises in Adult Life. New York: Dutton, 1976.

Sherman, Julia A., and Beck, Evelyn Torton, The Prism of Sex: Essays in the Sociology of Knowledge. Madison: University of Wisconsin Press, 1979.

Thomas, Alice, and Klassen, Dan, College Student Experiences and Quality of Effort at St. Olaf College: Preliminary Report. Office of Educational Research, St. Olaf College, Northfield, Minnesota, July, 1980.

Trilling, Lionel, Beyond Culture: Essays in Literature and Learning. New York, Harcourt, Brace, Janovich, 1965.

Trimble, John, Writing With Style: Conversations on the Art of Writing. Englewood Cliffs, N.J.: Prentice-Hall, 1975.

Troth, Audrey, and Farland, Ronnald, "The Development of Intellectual Orientations." Office of Educational Research, St. Olaf College, Northfield, Minnesota, November, 1973.

Weisel, Elie, Night. New York: Bantam, 1982.

Wilson, R.C. and Gaff, J.G. and others, <u>College Professors</u> <u>and</u> <u>Their</u> <u>Impact</u> <u>on</u> <u>Students</u>. New York: Wiley, 1975.

Whitehead, A.N. <u>The</u> <u>Aims</u> <u>of</u> <u>Education</u>. London: Williams and Norgate, 1951.

ABOUT THE AUTHOR

Wes Brown's interest in alternative higher education began when he worked as Director of the Methodist Student Movement at the University of the Pacific in the 1960's. Those were turbulent years in higher education, prompting attempts such as UOP's cluster colleges to make undergraduate education more humane, coherent, and effective. Convinced that colleges needed to do a better job meeting the developmental needs of students, he enrolled in graduate study with Nevitt Sanford at the Graduate Theological Union and at The University of California, Berkeley. He earned the PhD from the GTU in 1972, with a concentration in the social psychology of higher education, writing a dissertation on the effects of different types of academic institutions on the personal and professional development of faculty. His interest in innovative liberal education led to his appointment to the faculty of a new college, Hawaii Loa College in Kaheohe, Hawaii, where for eight years he taught psychology and served at various times as Dean of Academic Affairs, and Vice - President and Dean of Students. He served one year as Interim President of the Wright Institute, Berkeley, before accepting an appointment as Senior Tutor of the Paracollege at St. Olaf College, Northfield, Minnesota, a position he held for six years. He continues to teach psychology and religion at St Olaf in the Psychology Department and in the Paracollege, and to serve as a consultant to other institutions.